Holy Solitude

Lenten Reflections with Saints, Hermits, Prophets, and Rebels

HEIDI HAVERKAMP

WESTMINSTER
JOHN KNOX PRESS
LOUISVILLE • KENTUCKY

With honor and love for my mother,
Wenche Nilsen Haverkamp, 1942–2016,
who dearly loved her moments of solitude.

First edition
Published by Westminster John Knox Press
Louisville, Kentucky

17 18 19 20 21 22 23 24 25 26—10 9 8 7 6 5 4 3 2 1

Author photo by Adam Frieberg and used by permission.

Book design by Drew Stevens
Cover design by designpointinc.com

Library of Congress Cataloging-in-Publication Data
Names: Haverkamp, Heidi.
Title: Holy solitude : Lenten reflections with saints, hermits, prophets, and rebels / Heidi Haverkamp.
Description: Louisville, KY : Westminster John Knox Press, 2017. | Includes bibliographical references. |
Identifiers: LCCN 2017042868 (print) | LCCN 2017043078 (ebook) | ISBN 9781611648478 (ebk.) | ISBN 9780664263157 (pbk. : alk. paper)
Subjects: LCSH: Lent. | Spiritual exercises. | Spiritual life—Christianity.
Classification: LCC BV85 (ebook) | LCC BV85 .H425 2017 (print) | DDC 248.4/7—dc23
LC record available at https://lccn.loc.gov/2017042868

Most Westminster John Knox Press books are available at special quantity discounts when purchased in bulk by corporations, organizations, and special-interest groups. For more information, please e-mail SpecialSales@wjkbooks.com.

CONTENTS

INTRODUCTION

True solitude is the home of the person.
—Thomas Merton,
New Seeds of Contemplation

Always visualize your soul as vast, spacious, and plentiful.
—Teresa of Avila, *The Interior Castle*

*The LORD is good to those who wait for him,
to the soul that seeks him.*
—Lamentations 3:25

In my first years as a parish priest, I was completely over-whelmed. I found some relief for the stress by talking with my husband, seeing a therapist, going to yoga, and cooking. I also found solace in reading many, many books about hermits: Thomas Merton, May Sarton, Julian of Norwich, and many others, lesser known (see the Further Reading list for more details). I read about Carthusian monks and Orthodox *startsy*. I combed real estate websites in search of tiny houses for sale. I spent time alone at retreat centers for a night or two. Parish life was busy, noisy, and fragmented, so I fantasized about living all alone in a tiny house somewhere, where it was just me and God. (Thankfully, my husband didn't take this personally.)

Living alone in a little house is a fantasy I've had at many times in my life. When I was little, one of my daydreams was that I would grow up and live in a little cottage all by myself. In my early twenties, I lived in a one-room cabin in rural New England for a year and loved every minute of it, even waking up in the middle of the night all winter to throw another log into the woodstove.

I had the chance to live as an almost-hermit for a month as part of a sabbatical in 2014. I stayed in a hermitage on the grounds of the monastery where I'm an oblate. I read, napped, cooked, walked, wrote, and went to the liturgy of the hours every day. It wasn't total solitude, because I regularly shared meals with the sisters and a local friend, I used social media twice a week, I went to a prairie workday and a workshop on prayer, and I saw a spiritual director.

Although I savored those days and hours that spread out before me like an open road, I also fumbled and fidgeted with so much freedom. I'd move the hermitage furniture around for better "flow." I spent a lot of time at the grocery store and at Target, chasing after things I thought I needed: brown sugar, an extra throw pillow, a colander, knitting needles. I didn't have much of a spiritual framework for using my solitude. I threw myself into the thrill of an open schedule and introverted bliss, but I hadn't read enough of the desert fathers and mothers, Teresa of Avila, or other experts. Thankfully, the daily office with the sisters and the manual labor of preparing my own meals helped structure the days, but something was missing. One night, with less than a week left in my stay, I got spooked, and the very next day moved into the monastery guesthouse, where other people were sleeping right down the hall.

Scripture does not generally encourage solitude:

Woe to one who is alone and falls and does not have another to help. Again, if two lie together, they keep warm; but how can one keep warm alone? (Eccl. 4:10b–11)

The one who lives alone is self-indulgent,
    showing contempt for all who have sound
        judgment.
                                                    (Prov. 18:1)

Admittedly, at that time, it was important to be part of a clan, tribe, or household because being alone was dangerous. Encountering God, however, was usually a solitary encounter, experienced, for instance, by Abraham, Hagar, Jacob, Moses, Elijah, Jesus, Peter, and Paul. However, God's presence was somewhat dangerous too—rarely quiet or restful—more often intrusive, corrective, and even aggressive. Many people quote the verse, "Be still, and know that I am God!" (Ps. 46:10) in peaceful moments, without realizing the violence of the verse that comes before: "he breaks the bow, and shatters the spear; / he burns the shields with fire" (46:9). Stillness with God in scripture wasn't always tranquil, but it was certainly always life-transforming.

Jesus had a different relationship with solitude, compared to others in the Bible. His first time of holy solitude was very deliberate. The Gospel writers recount that before Jesus' public ministry, he went alone into the wilderness, where he spent forty days in prayer and fasting. There, his life-transforming encounter was not only with God, but with Satan. (Early desert fathers and mothers, too, encountered demons and the Evil One in their solitude. Perhaps I did in my hermitage, too, on that night I got spooked.) Later in his ministry, Jesus' relationship with solitude is more recognizable to modern people; he takes breaks. All four Gospel writers noticed Jesus' habit of taking time by himself: to pray, to recover from the travails of ministry, and in Mark and Luke, to grieve the death of his cousin John the Baptist.

Even though more and more people live alone nowadays, life-giving, healthy solitude isn't something we talk about much. *Being alone* sounds sad, aimless, or lonely, to hear ads or memes describe it. *Solitude*, however, is chosen and purposeful. It isn't loneliness, but the practice of a deep integrity. It's learning to be present to God wholeheartedly, as your true and simple self. Richard Foster wrote, "Loneliness is inner emptiness. Solitude is inner fulfillment."[1] There is an opening in the heart and mind in solitude that frees the soul to notice, listen, and reflect on the existence of God beyond and in all things, including the self. Teresa of Avila teaches in *The Interior Castle* that this awareness will grow into love: love of God, love of self, and love of neighbor. Solitude isn't about escape or introversion but about greater love; solitude creates space within us for God and all that is most important to us.

Solitude can be revolutionary. According to the world's standards, it means wasting time, doing "nothing." Taking time to be with God in solitude means stepping outside what is measurable, discovering "that being is more important than having and that we are worth more than the result of our efforts."[2] Moments of solitude can be for Christians what the Sabbath is for Jews—a time when nothing is consumed, produced, or achieved, but we are free and privileged to simply rest in the presence of God. As Walter Brueggemann points out in his book, *Sabbath as Resistance*, "YHWH is a Sabbath-keeping God, which fact ensures that restfulness and not restlessness is at the center of life."[3] He points to the words of Jesus, who taught: "Come to me, all you that are weary and are carrying heavy burdens, and I will give you rest" (Matt. 11:28); not, "I will give you more work." It's a radical choice to see and value your life in the way God does, that our being is more important than our doing. That doesn't mean that our doing isn't important at all but that the quality of our being is the foundation of our doing, as well as our serving, loving, dying, and rising again—in the same way it was for Jesus.

I don't read books about hermits or shop for tiny houses (much) anymore, but moments of solitude are the bread and butter that keep me going. God didn't create everyone with that same need, but if you've picked up this book, I imagine there's some hunger for solitude in you, too. Healthy solitude is not an escape or an end unto itself but a way to more deeply be yourself, allowing you to be more available to the presence of God and, in turn, to be available in a wholehearted and healthy way to the needs of other people.

This book is an attempt to share with you ways to reflect, deepen, and practice solitude as a fulsome Christian discipline, rooted in the Lenten journey of sacrifice and introspection and in the life, death, and resurrection of Jesus. The book is laid out thematically, exploring ways that other Christians have experienced solitude: listening, struggle, journey, hospitality, resistance, and confinement. Each day's devotion usually explores that theme through the life of a particular person, whether from Scripture or Christian history.

There are some concrete suggestions for practicing solitude: (1) on Sundays, I invite you to choose a practice for that week in light of its theme, and (2) on Fridays and Saturdays, I offer ways to push yourself further into inner solitude by practicing fasting and/or almsgiving. These two are ancient practices, especially used during Lent, that have stretched and enriched the lives of many Christians for generations, including most of the saints, hermits, prophets, and rebels I profile in this book. You may or may not feel up to them yourself this Lent, and that's fine; take them or leave them as seems right for you this year.

I want to leave you with the last paragraph of a bidding prayer for Lent from the Episcopal *Book of Common Prayer*. When I first heard it read in worship, probably in about 2002, it sounded strange and archaic to me, but now I find I'm inspired and humbled by it every year:

I invite you, therefore, in the name of the Church, to the observance of a holy Lent, by self-examination and repentance; by prayer, fasting, and self-denial; and by reading and meditating on God's holy Word. And, to make a right beginning of repentance, and as a mark of our mortal nature, let us now kneel before the Lord, our maker and redeemer.

Silence is then kept for a time.[4]

Heidi Haverkamp
Lent 2017

PREPARING FOR LENT

For which of you, intending to build a tower, does not first sit down and estimate the cost, to see whether he has enough to complete it?

—Luke 14:28

Keeping a holy Lent requires preparation. Practices and prayer suggested in this book will be easier to do if you take some time before the season to look at your calendar and do some scheduling in advance. Do some planning to prepare for your Lenten prayer life, fasting, and almsgiving, and to get your home ready for the season in the way you'd like.

This book focuses on the traditional Lenten discipline of prayer in the form of solitude, but I encourage you to try fasting and almsgiving as well. Abstaining from food (or other comforts) and giving away money are ways of probing both our vulnerability and our strength in Christ. Both can deepen into mindful solitude within us, making more space for trusting God and loving our neighbor.

PREPARING YOUR CALENDAR

So teach us to count our days
that we may gain a wise heart.
—Psalm 90:12

Modern life is busy. Plan ahead and put a few things on your calendar for Lent so that you are sure to make space for your spiritual life in the midst of everything else that will be demanding your attention. Strive to attend church on Sundays and holy days even if you are going to be out of town. Make a point of putting them on your calendar, being sure to check your church's website or newsletter for the right time and place. I encourage you to include:

— Ash Wednesday
— Maundy Thursday
— Good Friday
— Easter Vigil / Easter Sunday

Activities Suggested in This Book

— Mark Fridays as special fasting days; indicate the particular manner of fast for each Friday so that you can be ready and schedule around it as needed
— A retreat day; overnight or all day (in Week One, but can take place at any time)
— A long walk or a hike (in Week Two)
— Appointment with a pastor, priest, or close friend for a confession of sins (in Week Three)
— Visit to a crowded place for prayer and solitude for 20–60 minutes, perhaps over lunch (in Week Four)

Common Lenten Practices

— Holy Week or Palm Sunday weekend: time to prepare for Easter with cooking, shopping, flowers, and decorations
— Holy Week: dying eggs, which can be fun for both kids and adults (For a change of pace, see appendix B for a recipe to dye eggs dark red using onion skins, according to an Orthodox tradition.)
— Holy Saturday: time to remove any Lenten home decorations you may have used and to reset for Easter

PREPARING FOR FASTING

"And whenever you fast, do not look dismal, like the hypocrites, for they disfigure their faces so as to show others that they are fasting. Truly I tell you, they have received their reward. But when you fast, put oil on your head and wash your face, so that your fasting may be seen not by others but by your Father who is in secret; and your Father who sees in secret will reward you."

—Matthew 6:16–18

Fasting appears gloomy until one steps into its arena. But begin and you will see what light it brings after darkness, what freedom from bonds, what release after a burdensome life . . .

—Theophan the Recluse[1]

Fasting creates a kind of solitude within us, an emptiness that many Christians throughout history have found makes more room inside them for God, grace, and guidance. In my early thirties, I became curious about fasting.

The ancient mystics and desert mothers and fathers I read were devoted to it, but I'd never heard it talked about in church. In seminary, I met with Father Robert Koomson, a warm, elder Ghanaian man who was our chaplain; twice, I went to him for spiritual direction, and twice, he recommended fasting to me. The second time, he gave me a copy of a slim book he had written on the subject, published in his home country. I've since misplaced it, but the clarity and confidence of the simple lessons he wrote about fasting have stayed with me. (For instance, it helps to drink warm water to settle your grumbly stomach.) When we long for clarity from God or about any other matter in life or are dealing with pain, loss, or a broken relationship, Father Koomson recommends fasting combined with prayer. I tried fasting for years and mostly felt hungry and grumpy. The problem was that I was doing the fasting part but not the praying part. The two have to go together, or it's a waste of your time and a bellyache.

You may or may not feel ready to include fasting as part of your Lenten practice this year. The most basic kind of Lenten fast is to deprive yourself of something—a certain food or other comfort. Going without a meal or fasting for an entire day requires a bit more care. In this book, I invite you to try fasting from a meal or two as a special Friday fast; more than that, I encourage you to see a spiritual director or find a book that teaches fasting. (Since Father Koomson's book is not available in the United States, I recommend two texts in the Further Reading list.) Remember that the purpose of a Lenten discipline is to follow Jesus into the wilderness for forty days—to grow in our relationship with God by stretching ourselves spiritually—not to punish ourselves or live in misery for seven weeks.

If you choose to try it, remember that fasting is about God's grace, not human endurance. If you slip up in your fast—and if you're anything like me, you will—don't give up! Keep trying. Remember that, traditionally, Sundays are a feast day, so they're exempt from the forty days and you can take a break. Finally, remember that your Lenten fast is between you and God. As much as you can manage it, don't reveal your fasting to others. The sixth chapter of Matthew, read at most Ash Wednesday services, makes clear that fasting is private and not something to broadcast or make a big deal out of. On the other hand, there is no need to be cagey or secretive. Fasting is for you and God, but there may be times when neighbor love or hospitality calls for you to break your fast in order to share a special meal or be part of a special gathering.

In this book, you'll be invited to do additional fasting on Fridays, as Christians have done since ancient times to meditate on the mystery of the Crucifixion. You may choose to do some, none, or all of those special fasting days. If you slip up and forget or are unable to overcome temptation, remember that you haven't lost the whole day: try to get back in the saddle instead of chucking the fast entirely. Fasting is about you and God, not endurance or "being good." Fasting can help us grow in dependence on God, in solidarity with the hungry and needy, and in making space and solitude inside us for prayer and listening, which we may otherwise fill with food, noise, shopping, or other comforts. Consider giving it a try!

PREPARING FOR ALMSGIVING

Prayer with fasting is good, but better than both is almsgiving with righteousness. A little with righteousness is better than wealth with wrongdoing. It is better to give alms than to lay up gold.

—Tobit 12:8

When you give alms, do not let your left hand know what your right hand is doing.

—Matthew 6:3

Almsgiving can also create solitude within us by helping us let go of money and its security. It's an ancient Lenten practice. Giving money to the poor, whether into the cups of panhandlers or writing checks to charity, opens our grip and makes more space in us for our neighbor and God's presence, which, in the end, is the only security we have.

In this book, on each Saturday, I suggest practicing one of two forms of almsgiving:

1. Give cash on the spot—to a panhandler, to kids from a local school raising money at a stoplight, to a charity box on a store counter, to a tip jar, or to whatever "ask" God may place in your path. Do not judge the person or group asking; just give, trusting in God's grace.
2. Give to an organization—write a check or give online to a charity that is meaningful to you. Each Saturday, I include a reflection piece to help you consider potential recipients in the spirit of that week's devotions.

Each Saturday, choose one or the other, or do both. Do some planning for this in advance: discern in advance the amount you'll give each weekend so that you can budget and have cash on hand as needed. Choose an amount to give away each weekend, depending on your normal weekly expenses: one dollar, five dollars, ten, twenty, fifty, or even one hundred dollars. The amount should stretch your generosity, not bankrupt you but make you wince a bit. (If you are not wincing, go a denomination higher!) You should choose one dollar only if you are a minimum-wage worker or otherwise living in poverty. For "cash on the spot," if you are like me and do not use much cash, you may want to go the bank and withdraw five to seven bills to have in reserve for each of the seven Saturdays of Lent.

I am amazed and a bit ashamed when I notice that I will spend more on items for myself than I am likely to give to charity or put in the offering plate at church. Almsgiving reminds us that all we own belonged to God before it belonged to us. Still, it's hard to give money away when we don't receive something in return. Giving to a charity is probably the best use of your alms, but there is something that hits you in the gut when you put a wad of cash in a tip jar or in the hand of a panhandler. It begins to open a space within, where perhaps God can be even more generous to you.

In preparation for this book, I handed out one ten-dollar bill a week for six weeks, usually to a beggar but also into a tip jar or two. I was surprised by both how hard and how easy it was. It made me notice how tightly I clutch what I believe is *mine.* Also, with each "giveaway," I noticed it felt good—even fun—to be generous and to utterly delight someone who is not used to receiving much at all, even if a panhandler or barista went and spent my (my?) money on drugs or alcohol. (One priest I know says to his congregation with regards to panhandlers: "I mean, I spend the money you give me on drugs and alcohol, too.")

PREPARING AT HOME

Prepare your work outside,
get everything ready for you in the field;
and after that build your house.
— Proverbs 24:27

Write [God's words] on the doorposts of your house and on
your gates.
— Deuteronomy 11:20

At my house, for years I changed almost nothing for Lent, even though I like to decorate for other liturgical seasons, like Advent, Christmas, and Easter. Lent is one of the most meaningful seasons of the year to me; I wanted a way to reset my home so that I would remember every day that

I was in the midst of a special and particular time. Your practice of solitude can be enhanced every day if, when you look around your home, you are reminded of Lent and your Lenten intentions. Consider one or more of the following suggestions or experiment with your own ideas.

Tabletop Desert

Fill a bowl with sand. Add a stone, a nail, and maybe even a toy snake or scorpion. Bury a small slip of paper with the word *Alleluia* on it. Set it somewhere you will see it regularly, maybe where you eat meals or on your work desk.

Tabletop Arrangements

Fill a vase, bowl, or bucket with bare sticks, dry flower stems, thistles, or other thorny branches. Wrap arrangements with materials like burlap, twine, and metal wire, brown or purple yarn or ribbon. On Palm Sunday, add any palms you bring home from church. Or set out a low bowl or pan and fill with gravel, pebbles, bits of metal, or pieces of bone.

Door Hangings

Hang an austere wreath on your door, perhaps of grapevine, twigs, straw, dried flowers, or rough fabrics like burlap or canvas. Grapevine wreaths can be found in most craft stores.

Display a Cross or Crucifix

Display a cross or crucifix in a highly visible place. Perhaps replace another art object that hangs in a prominent location in your home.

No Candles

Do not light any candles in your home until Easter Sunday. You may want to put them all away, out of sight.

Live Simply

Within reason, keep your shopping and leisure habits at their most basic. Choose the most simple, inexpensive options. When there is an option, choose the less fancy or special. If you can, try not to *buy* anything for the Lenten decorating of your home; use objects or materials that you find outside or lying around your house or at Goodwill.

Switch to Easter Decorations

On Holy Saturday, the day of emptiness and waiting, remove all Lenten things. Wait to replace with Easter decorations until Holy Saturday night or first thing Easter Sunday morning, to increase the suspense. (It's like Christmas morning but for Easter!)

FIRST DAYS OF LENT

ASH WEDNESDAY: THE INNER ROOM

"But you, when you pray, go into your inner room, close your door and pray to your Father who is in secret, and your Father who sees what is done in secret will reward you."
—Matthew 6:6 NASB

A certain brother went to Abbot Moses in Scete and asked him for a good word. And the elder said to him: Go, sit in your cell, and your cell will teach you everything.
—Thomas Merton, *The Wisdom of the Desert*

In the King James Bible, the "inner room" verse of Matthew 6 reads: "When thou prayest, enter thy closet." The Greek word *tameion* means "storage room"—a humble, quiet room with a few buckets and crates but probably no beautiful view or easy place to sit. Finding a place to be in the presence of God doesn't require much, Jesus seems to say. He is teaching, first, that prayer isn't a public performance or a way of showing others we're religious; at the same time, he wants us to realize the opposite—that prayer is a way to know God in a private and personal way. The inner room he mentions may not be a place in your physical home so much as inside yourself.

What is the inner room of the soul like? Catherine of Siena spoke of keeping a hermitage inside her heart. Francis of Assisi said, "Brother Body is our cell, and the soul is the hermit who remains inside the cell to pray to God and meditate."[1] Teresa of Avila wrote a book about prayer, *The Interior Castle*, named after the intricate extended metaphor she used to describe the soul. You can think of the inner room of your soul as a cozy house, a simple cell, or a "vast, spacious, and plentiful"[2] place. However you may like to imagine it, there's a place inside you where God is waiting to sit with you.

Abba Moses, also called Moses the Black, was a fourth-century desert father from Ethiopia who was a thief before he was a monk. He taught his monks that "your cell will teach you everything," as Merton quotes above, and he meant both the physical cell where a hermit was living (a cave or hut) and the inner, spiritual cell of solitude. Solitude invites us to sit not only in the presence of God but also with ourselves. There's no better way to get to know someone than to sit in a car with them for a while. The same is true of God and the self. It's not always easy to sit still with yourself or with God, especially for extended periods of time; but like a child resting in a parent's lap, sometimes just to sit together is enough.

Contemplation and solitude go together. Thomas Merton described it as "life itself, fully awake, fully active, fully aware that it is alive. It is spiritual wonder. It is spontaneous awe at the sacredness of life, of being. It is gratitude for life, for awareness and for being."[3] This Lent, like many saints, hermits, prophets, and rebels before you, you're going to spend some intentional time in solitude and, I hope, get to know God's love more deeply and enter more fully into Jesus' Passion and Resurrection by doing so.

Questions for Reflection

1. What image do you prefer for the inner room of the soul: cell, closet, hermitage, or castle? Why? Is there a term you do not like? Why?
2. Have you ever thought of Lent as a contemplative season before? What about Lent, specifically, could be called contemplative?
3. What made you pick up this book? What do you hope to gain from using it for Lent this year?

Choose a Practice for This Week

— Observe the ancient tradition of fasting on Ash Wednesday. Skip either lunch or dinner. Sip tea or water to ease hunger pains. Use those twinges as a call to prayer and to "remember you are dust and to dust you shall return."
— Find twenty to thirty minutes of quiet solitude. Ask the Holy Spirit to guide and speak to you through drawing. Draw either your inner room or your "interior castle." If you have time, or at another time this week, draw your "wilderness" as it feels at this season of your life. If you would prefer, you can describe these things with words instead of drawing.

# THURSDAY: THE WILDERNESS

He was in the wilderness forty days, tempted by Satan; and he was with the wild beasts.

—Mark 1:13

And I say, "O that I had wings like a dove!
I would fly away and be at rest;
truly, I would flee far away;
I would lodge in the wilderness.

—Psalm 55:6–8

We must cross the desert and spend some time in it to receive
the grace of God as we should. It is there that one empties
oneself, that one drive away from oneself everything that is
not God and that one empties completely the small house of
one's soul so as to leave all the room free for God alone. . . .
It is indispensable: the soul needs the silence of it, the inward
retirement, this oblivion of all created things.
—Charles de Foucauld, as quoted in Sara Maitland,
A Book of Silence

Going out into the wilderness is just the opposite of entering into your inner room: there are open vistas and rough
terrain instead of an enclosed, private space. In the wilderness, solitude is less about intimacy with God and more
about spiritual awe and freedom. Going into the wilderness is also an act of vulnerability: there is danger from
weather, snakes, scorpions, and other wild animals, or just
in finding enough to eat and drink.

Jesus was probably seeking both awe and danger when
he went out into the Judean wilderness for forty days
before his public ministry. He went to pray in the freedom
of solitude and to be alone with God. He also went to test
himself. Alone in the starkness and quiet of the desert, he
must have wrestled with his deepest questions about his
humanity and his divinity and about what it was that God
was calling him to do. The desert took away all barriers
between his soul and God's wide gaze, which must have
been thrilling but also quite strenuous.

There is a long tradition in scripture of faithful people
going alone into the wilderness and encountering God,

including Hagar, Moses, Elijah, and John the Baptist, among others. The Israelites spent forty years as a people alone with God, out in the desert. Early Christians continued this tradition when untold numbers of men and women left society to live with God in the wilderness, especially in the deserts of Egypt but in places all around the Mediterranean, following in the footsteps of the first desert solitary, Antony the Great (see Week Two). These desert mothers and fathers discovered, as Jesus did, that both God and the Devil, or demons, wait for us in solitude.

There is something about wilderness that draws prayer from us, whether in wonder, discernment, help, or lament. There is something about wild places that invites spiritual solitude; where, in spite of ourselves, as Foucauld says in the quotation above: "one empties completely the small house of one's soul so as to leave all the room free for God alone." We cannot help but feel vulnerable and exposed in the wilderness. It is a place for both awe and humility.

If Lent is a time for us to imitate Jesus' forty days in the desert, then it should be less a time to suffer and endure and more a time to grow in this kind of wonder and vulnerability. Engaging in prayer, fasting, and almsgiving are not about punishment; they help us transcend ourselves—finding greater intimacy with God and greater clarity about who we are. These three practices are also disciplines of solitude, forms of self-denial or self-emptying to make more room in us for God. Prayer reveals our emotional and spiritual vulnerability; fasting reveals our physical and psychological vulnerability; almsgiving reveals our material and financial vulnerability. In the wilderness and on the cross, Jesus made himself vulnerable, too—even unto death.

Lent is a wilderness set in time. In it, whether or not we are living anywhere near a physical wilderness or in a wilderness time of life, we can choose to live starkly and mindfully, in a way set apart from the rest of the year and the rest of human society. Even if you do not leave your hometown in the next seven weeks, you can find ways to "flee far away [and] lodge in the wilderness," and there encounter God.

Questions for Reflection

1. When you go on vacation, do you enjoy traveling to wilderness places? What about the wilderness draws you? Or what is it about the wilderness that doesn't hold much interest for you?
2. When have you had a time of wilderness in your life where you met God in a new and powerful way?
3. Is there a wilderness in your life right now that is pushing you to prayer? How would you describe it? Are your prayers of wonder, discernment, help, or lament?

⚱ FRIDAY FASTING: THIRST

Drink Only Water (Eat as Usual)

O God, you are my God, I seek you,
my soul thirsts for you;
my flesh faints for you,
as in a dry and weary land where there is no water.
—Psalm 63:1

Jesus said to her, "Everyone who drinks of this water will be thirsty again, but those who drink of the water that I will give them will never be thirsty. The water that I will give will become in them a spring of water gushing up to eternal life."
—John 4:13–14

Inspiration

Drinking nothing but tepid or warm water is a small way to begin to fast. You're practicing an emptiness of your body, growing in awareness of your thirst (what are you *really* thirsty for, if you have plenty of water to drink?), and growing in awareness and compassion for people who truly are in want of clean, plentiful water. By making a water fast, you can really notice the empty, thirsty places within you and purposefully invite God into them: your own inner deserts in need of God's living water. This is an incarnate solitude!

Practice

Drink only water, without ice and without flavoring. Hot or warm water is okay. Decide if you can realistically go without caffeine; if not, adjust accordingly. You may want to carry a water bottle with you in case only iced or chilled water is available in restaurants, your workplace, or school. Every time you crave something besides plain water to drink or you feel irritated or unsatisfied by it, remember and offer prayers for those who may not have clean water at all. Ask God: What am I *truly* thirsting for in my life right now?

If at all possible, do not announce or reveal your fast to others outside your immediate family, if even them. If you want, keep your fast for the whole weekend. If you're feeling the need of an even greater challenge, keep your "water only" fast until next Friday.

Questions for Reflection

1. How did it feel to quench only your thirst and not to drink for pleasure?
2. Did you notice your thirst in a different way? Did you drink more or less than you usually would?

3. Did it help you deepen in solitude with God, or was it just inconvenient?

# SATURDAY ALMSGIVING: CONGREGATIONS

I was glad when they said to me,
"Let us go to the house of the LORD!"
—Psalm 122:1

In him the whole structure is joined together and grows into a holy temple in the Lord; in whom you also are built together spiritually into a dwelling place for God.
—Ephesians 2:21–22

Choose the form of almsgiving you will practice this week or, if it gives you joy, do both. Give an amount that feels generous and "hurts" a little in the context of your weekly expenses. Grow in solitude by giving to others.

1. Give cash away to someone who asks you for it.
2. Mail a check, give online, or put your gift in the offering plate tomorrow for a congregation.

One of the most important centers of your spiritual life is the congregation you call home. Its sanctuary is a particular "inner room" and, hopefully, a shelter for your soul. Congregations are only as strong as the generosity and joy of their members. Make a special Lenten gift to your congregation or to any other congregation that is meaningful for you:
— the congregation you attend now
— the congregation where you grew up or where you feel you really became a Christian

— a congregation that is taking very good care of someone you love right now
— a mosque, synagogue, or other religious or spiritual center in your community

Questions for Reflection

1. Does generosity make you feel rich or poor this week? Does it feel like a spiritual act?
2. How did you choose where to give your alms this week?
3. Did giving make more space within you for the presence of God? How?

WEEK ONE

SOLITUDE AND SILENCE

SUNDAY: LISTENING TO SILENCE

For God alone my soul waits in silence;
from him comes my salvation.
He alone is my rock and my salvation,
my fortress; I shall never be shaken.
— Psalm 62:1–2

True silence is the search of man for God. . . . True silence
is a garden enclosed, where alone the soul can meet its
God. . . . True silence is a key to the immense and flaming
heart of God.
— Catherine Doherty, *Poustinia: Encountering God*
in Solitude, Silence and Prayer

One year, I tried giving up listening to music and radio news for Lent. After a week, I was going nuts. The idea that I was going to have to stick with this deafening quiet for six more weeks did not help, so I quit. Maybe I proved my own weakness, which some say is the point of Lent, but maybe I failed because I didn't add anything to replace what music and news were providing in my daily life. I could have filled all that empty audio space with intercessory prayer, singing out loud to myself, conversations with God, and phone calls to family or friends. I love silence, but that particular Lenten silence was nothing more than an endurance test: there was no deeper spiritual learning or understanding to my practice that could've helped me grow in my relationship with God.

Life-giving, contemplative silence is not just the lack of noise; it is the audio space to feel that Something More is deeply present and deeply loves you. The point is not sterile quiet but the sense that there is Something to listen for. Quakers have called this the "sacrament of silence" and practiced it together for centuries. We might call it, in the spirit of *The Book of Common Prayer*'s definition of a sacrament, "an outer and *audible* sign of an inward and spiritual grace."[4]

When most people find themselves walking out into a beautiful spot in the natural world or sitting in an empty church or other sacred place, the deep stillness and silence feels moving and profound, often even for people of no religious tradition. There is transcendence—a feeling of mystery and love—in this kind of silence. Thomas Merton wrote that churches should always be left open for all to come and find this kind of stillness: "A place where your mind can be idle, and forget its concerns, descend into silence, and worship the Father in secret."[5] His words echo the "praying in secret" of Matthew 6; we can find our inner room in large sacred spaces of silence just as we can in the silence of a cozy room or hermitage. Even in the midst of a busy day or an otherwise normal worship service, a moment of silence and quiet can open a door to the presence of God. At my

last church, during the Sunday evening service, three minutes of silence followed the homily. Attenders of that service often told me it was their favorite time of the week;
one man once remarked to me, "It is more profound than
the greatest Bach chorale or the most astounding sermon!"

It can be both awkward and wondrous spending
extended time in silence and solitude. It is easy to get fidg-
ety. Sometimes keeping it simple makes the difference for
me; just to look out a window for a while or to notice the
pause of a moment in time.

Ruth Burrows, an English Carmelite nun, writes that
prayer, especially in silence, is simpler than we think,
because it "is essentially what *God* does, how God addresses
us, looks at us. It is not primarily something we are doing
to God, something we are giving to God but what God
is doing for us. And what God is doing for us is giving
us the divine Self in love."[6] The real discipline of solitude
and silence is to let go of our preconceptions and distractions, to let God love us—even just for a moment—and
to remember that this is the most important practice and
nourishment for Christian life, each and every day.

Questions for Reflection

1. What has been your relationship with silence? What
   circumstances make silence a "sacrament" for you or
   a time you can feel loved by God? What can make it
   awkward or unsettling for you?
2. Have you noticed "moments of silence" in your everyday
   life before? Perhaps waiting at an elevator, standing in
   line at the store, waiting for the microwave to beep, or
   noticing the sudden quiet after you turn off a television
   or finish a phone call. Have you ever used a moment like
   this to be aware of God's presence with you and God's
   love for you? How could you remind yourself to try this?
3. Consider turning off sources of background sound
   in the course of your day. For instance, in your car,

around your home, during meals, or when you exercise. Use the silence as a space to practice feeling God's presence and love around and within you. Have a conversation with God, as you would a friend or spouse. (The Friday Fast this week will invite you to do this for a whole day.)

Choose a Practice for This Week

— Spend time in silent solitude once a day. Spend three to five minutes alone, sitting still, in as quiet a place as you can find. You might want to go into a bathroom, if choices are limited, or per Matthew 6, a *tameion* or closet. Do nothing; just sit, breathe, and listen.

— Schedule a day of silence and solitude for yourself. If at all possible, arrange to be away from home overnight or at least for several hours. If you cannot afford a retreat center, your pastor will probably let you spend the day at your church. If you want to do what Catherine Doherty proscribes (see Tuesday's devotion for details) and your health permits, eat only bread and drink only water, coffee, or tea during this time. Bring only paper, a pen, and a Bible. You could also bring a cross or an icon of Mary. Napping is a perfectly fine way to pray, by the way. If you cannot manage a quiet day this week, look ahead on your calendar and schedule it for later.

MONDAY: ELIJAH ON MOUNT HOREB

[The LORD] said, "Go out and stand on the mountain before the LORD, for the LORD is about to pass by." Now there was a great wind, so strong that it was splitting mountains and breaking rocks in pieces before the LORD, but the LORD was

not in the wind; and after the wind an earthquake, but the
LORD was not in the earthquake; and after the earthquake
a fire, but the LORD was not in the fire; and after the fire a
sound of sheer silence. When Elijah heard it, he wrapped his
face in his mantle and went out and stood at the entrance of
the cave. Then there came a voice to him that said, "What
are you doing here, Elijah?"

—1 Kings 19:11–13

Elijah walked alone for forty days through the desert wilderness, from Beersheba to Mount Horeb, the mountain in Egypt where God gave Moses the Ten Commandments. We aren't entirely sure of its location, but some traditional maps put his journey at over 250 miles. He was leaving in his wake two tremendous works of faith: he'd ended a terrible drought, and he'd lit a soaking wet altar of wood and dead ox into a raging fire, shaming the failed attempts of the prophets of Baal, favorites of Queen Jezebel. In accordance with the law of that time,[7] Elijah killed all 450 of them.

Then, he fled for the hills, fearing the queen's revenge. He must have been exhausted, maybe even in shock after causing so much bloodshed. In Beersheba, he left his servant behind and continued on, alone. Sustained by an angel, he walked for forty days and nights to Horeb. Once there, like Moses, he hid himself in a cave on the mountainside, overlooking the vast Egyptian desert and sky. There, the voice of God found him.

Most of us don't hear God audibly speaking to us, even on silent retreats or remote hiking trips like Elijah's. In solitude, though, there is a space that opens inside and around us and makes us more available to encounter God or hear God speaking in a way we would not otherwise. Like Elijah on his solo journey, while solitude can leave us vulnerable to both physical and spiritual danger, that same vulnerability can also make space in us for God, space that might otherwise be filled with busyness, entertainment, or the ordinary demands of life.

Go out on top of the mountain and wait for me, Elijah heard in the cave. He would have remembered that Moses experienced the divine presence on that very same mountain, when God hid him "in a cleft of the rock" and passed by (Exod. 33:21–23). But Elijah was told to stand *out on top* of the mountain, where there was no hiding place. When Elijah obeyed, he found himself confronted with a terrible wind, a ferocious earthquake, and a burst of fire. It was at "a sound of sheer silence" (1 Kgs. 19:12), however, when he covered his face and fell back to the mouth of the cave.

It was then that God asked him, "What are you doing here, Elijah?" (1 Kgs. 19:9).

Questions for Reflection

1. What draws you to solitude? Elijah was exhausted, in danger, and perhaps fed up with all God had asked him to do. Have you ever felt like this? Or does something else drive you to spend time alone?
2. Have you had an experience of God in "the sheer sound of silence"? What was it like? Were you alone or with others? Did you feel cared for by God? Challenged?
3. If you heard God's voice ask "What are you doing here?" today, how would you respond?

TUESDAY: MARY THE *THEOTOKOS*

But she was much perplexed by his words and pondered what sort of greeting this might be.

—Luke 1:29

But Mary treasured all these words and pondered them in her heart.

—Luke 2:19

There may be no one in the world who knows more about the miracles that can happen in silence and solitude than a pregnant woman. Mary carried Jesus in her body, in deep, incarnate silence, for nine months. Astounding to imagine, she would have felt the Word of God quickening in her womb. She knew the Savior was coming into the world before anyone else did. She held and grew the *Logos* inside herself. In Orthodox Christianity, she is called *Theotokos*, the God-bearer.

We don't all have wombs and we won't all give birth or have children, but like Mary, we can all be Christ-bearers. We can make space for the love of Christ inside our bodies, hearts, and minds. This is a physical, almost literal, interpretation of that "inner room" of Matthew 6: that we not only pray to Christ from inside the private room of the self but that we carry and bear him there always, like the pregnant Mary.

In silence, we can become aware of the inner spaces of our bodies. The noise and distractions of life may keep us stuck in the mind: problem-solving, making lists, navigating places and people outside ourselves. Coming to a full stop in solitude and silence can allow your mind to descend into your body and heart. What is it like to grow an awareness of your inner rooms, your "interior castle," as Teresa of Avila described it? You can become more aware of your breathing, remembering that the Holy Spirit moves through you as breath (*pneuma* in Greek and *ruah* in Hebrew mean both "breath" and "spirit"). Meditate on the goodness of your body—each limb, organ, and cell— remembering that God created you, flesh and spirit, and knows every hair of your head. Spending time in solitude and silence allows you to become more familiar with the sensations and the fact of your body—its strengths, wonders, emotions, and pains—and so then to navigate your exterior life with greater awareness. The Spirit speaks to us through the sensations of the body: our longings, fears, and fury. We feel love—from God and people—primarily as an incarnate reality, inside our bodies.

Luke tells us that Mary pondered and meditated on the messages from God that came to her from the angels and shepherds. Being a bearer of Christ does not mean that we've figured it all out or have an unshakable faith. Mary herself wondered and pondered: What did this all mean? What was happening? She wasn't sure, but she made room for the mystery of God inside herself, and it transformed her—body and soul. We can ponder the Holy and know that the presence of God will come and dwell in us simply *because* we are pondering and wondering. Inviting God to dwell within you is as simple as being aware that God already is. Paul told the Corinthians, "Do you not know that you are God's temple and that God's Spirit dwells in you?" (1 Cor. 3:16).

Like a pregnant woman, trust that tremendous things can happen within you in silence and solitude, even though it can seem to the outside world as though nothing is happening. Like a pregnant woman, what grows inside us when we make room within for God's presence is love—love in Christ, who longs to bless us with grace and new life, especially in this Lenten season of preparing for resurrection.

Questions for Reflection

1. How is Christ seeking to grow in love and new life within you—even within your body—this Lent?
2. What would it be like to think of the time you spend pondering, wondering, or questioning as time spent in prayer? What if doing these things is a way of opening yourself to being loved by God?

WEDNESDAY:
WHEN GOD IS SILENT

I cry to you and you do not answer me;
I stand, and you merely look at me.
—Job 30:20

Lord, why are you silent?
—Sebastião Rodrigues,
Silence

And about three o'clock Jesus cried with a loud voice, "Eli,
Eli, lema sabachthani?" that is, "My God, my God, why
have you forsaken me?"
—Matthew 27:46

No matter how long we sit in silence and solitude, sometimes God is the one who is silent. We may sit in quiet,
with a candle burning and beautiful music playing, and
feel nothing of the divine presence whatsoever. In fact,
choosing to spend more time in silence and solitude might
mean we more often feel that God is silent or absent.

It's hard to know why some people feel the presence of
God, some even constantly, while others struggle to feel
God's presence at all. A young parishioner once told me that
she didn't feel anything when she received Communion and
she wondered if she should. I wish I knew a proven method
to "feel" God's presence, but feeling a spiritual sense or
relationship like this is different for each person. It can
even feel different over the course of your life. One of the
most famous saints of the twentieth century, Mother Teresa
of Calcutta, after feeling a clear sense of the presence of
Christ, felt God's absence acutely—for decades. She wrote
in a letter, "even deep down, right in, there is nothing but
emptiness and darkness.—My God—how painful is this
unknown pain. It pains without ceasing."[8]

Scripture and the writings of many saints tell us that feeling as if God is silent or absent is not abnormal, even in a life of faith. Many psalms cry out at the silence of God (Pss. 10, 13, 22, 42). Job, in the midst of utter calamity and misery, felt that God was present—but silent. Job's greatest pain seems to have been that God did not offer any explanation of his terrible suffering (God did finally respond to Job but not with an explanation). Jesus cried out on the cross that God had abandoned him; even the Son of God felt the silence of God.

Feeling that God is silent or absent does not mean we have failed at faith or prayer. It does not mean that God is not with us. Mother Teresa came to see her feelings of abandonment and despair as a way to empathize more deeply with Jesus and the poor. In the novel, *Silence*, Father Rodrigues grappled with the absence of God in the face of the terrible suffering and deaths of the Japanese Christians he served. Eventually, Christ broke that silence, saying simply, "It was to share men's pain that I carried my cross."[9] Pain and abandonment are not feelings that can separate us from God in Christ or even from other human beings, because they are feelings we share.

Christ's suffering and death led to resurrection. God answered Job in a whirlwind. Mother Teresa is now Saint Theresa, and her struggle with doubt and darkness are now a source of comfort and hope for any and all of us who continue to struggle with these same things.

Questions for Reflection

1. Recall a time when you felt God was silent. How did you get through it? Was there any sense of redemption in your experience?
2. Read one of the psalms mentioned above. How does it speak to you as you practice silence and solitude this Lent?

3. What is it like to know that someone like Mother Teresa struggled so painfully with God's absence? Does it give you a feeling of comfort? Or disappointment?

THURSDAY: CATHERINE DOHERTY AND THE *POUSTINIA*

The poustinia *is a place where you are going to meet Christ in joyful solitude. . . .*
If there is anything the devil detests, it is the poustinia.
— Catherine Doherty, *Poustinia: Encountering God in Solitude, Silence and Prayer*

Catherine de Hueck was born in Russia and emigrated to Canada in 1921. She founded settlement houses in Toronto and New York City. In the 1940s, she married Eddie Doherty. They moved to rural Ontario, where a community of Roman Catholic laypeople formed around them. Madonna House still exists in Combermere, Ontario, with offshoot houses in many other places, welcoming guests and offering Doherty's teachings on simplicity, serving the poor, and prayer.

Doherty's faith was steeped in both religious traditions that formed her: Russian Orthodoxy, from her childhood, and Roman Catholicism, to which she converted as an adult. *Poustinia* in Russian means "desert," and in the Orthodox tradition, it also means a small house or room used for solitary prayer. Doherty introduced this spiritual discipline to Madonna House. She gave very specific directions for the bare furnishings of a *poustinia*: a large cross, an icon of Mary, a cot, a chair and table, a Bible, paper and pencil, and a loaf of bread. Mature Christians (as determined by a spiritual director) at Madonna House are invited to spend twenty-four hours in a *poustinia*, eating only bread, drinking only water, tea, or coffee, and reading only the Bible.

I admit that I didn't check with a spiritual director first, but before writing this book, I tried a day in a *poustinia*. It lightened my body to eat only bread and tea for a day, without the usual hunger pains I've known from a full fast. (But I daydreamed a lot about peanut butter and frozen custard.) The silent, unscheduled quiet of that day was actually harder than the diet. My brain searched out dozens of ways to distract itself: I was irritated by a hangnail, then I couldn't find nail clippers; I was too cold, then too hot; I made tea, but I spilled it all over the floor; I needed to move the furniture around; my mind spat out a never-ending list of things to do when I got home, which I tried to set them aside by writing a list for later, but it got pretty long.

Sometimes, I was able to give myself over to the presence of God. I read psalms, I listened to the birds and the leaves rustling in the trees, I wrote in my journal, I paced the room to focus my prayers, and I napped. Still, I made it only fifteen hours. Perhaps, like Antony the Great (see Week 2), little demons were poking and prodding me; but unlike those tormenting Antony, my little demons won, and I left the hermitage before my twenty-four hours were up. I broke my bread-and-water fast with a cheap take-out meal of a burger, French fries, and, yes, a frozen custard.

Spending a day in the silence of a *poustinia* — even if it's just a study room at the library or the guest room in your house — is both a penance and a delight. It's not as punishing as a hair shirt or walking a thousand miles to Jerusalem, but it's rigorous and revealing all the same. You are stuck with God and with yourself, cooped up with all your predilections, cravings, and pet peeves. There is a certain agony in being faced with nothing but yourself and God, even if it tends toward the ridiculous on the scale of agonies. It's also wondrous and joyful to be free to spend a day with the Almighty—as Doherty puts it, "we have a cup of coffee and I chew the fat with him."[10] It's hard to just be and to let yourself be loved by God without the cheap grace of frozen custard and to-do lists getting in the way—which is what makes it worth trying.

Questions for Reflection

1. Have you ever felt as though you were "having a cup of coffee" with God? If not, does it appeal to you? (Regardless of your choice of beverage.)
2. Do you feel nudged to try a *poustinia* day? Why or why not? What appeals and what doesn't? If you haven't already, consider scheduling an overnight stay somewhere or blocking out the better part of a day in your calendar to spend at a monastery, at your church, or even in a room at home, if you can keep yourself from chores or other distractions, to simply let God love you in your solitude.

 FRIDAY FASTING: SILENCE

Eliminate Noise

Physical solitude, exterior silence and real recollection are all morally necessary for anyone who wants to lead a contemplative life.
—Thomas Merton, *New Seeds of Contemplation*

The LORD is good to those who wait for him,
to the soul that seeks him.
It is good that one should wait quietly
for the salvation of the LORD.
                    —Lamentations 3:25–26

Inspiration

The movie *Into Great Silence* is a documentary about the lives of Carthusian monks. It's three hours long and contains almost no words. Carthusian monks live as hermits, but they also live in community as part of a large complex of hermitages and share in some worship and fellowship together. They don't take a vow of silence, but they live without talking much all the same. The movie captures the nuance, beauty, and fullness of their lives. You can see and *hear* the holy solitude of the monks in their daily life together.

How often are you barraged by human voices, music, the blips and beeps of your mobile device, or other noise that you can't turn off? This week, when you have a choice, choose silence and see what happens. Spend your Friday—or as much of it as you can—fasting from your usual audio life.

Practice

Fast from all noise that you are able to turn off or choose not to use: radio, television, podcasts, audio books, music, computer alerts and pings, your car horn, your phone ringer (if you need to be alerted to calls immediately, try the vibrate function). It may be difficult to adjust to so much quiet. You may find yourself feeling distracted or anxious. Notice if certain painful thoughts or worries surface repeatedly.

If at all possible, do not announce or reveal your fast to others outside your immediate family, if even them. If you want, keep you fast for the whole weekend. If you're

feeling the need of an even greater challenge, keep your
fast from noise until next Friday.

Questions for Reflection

1. What surprised you about trying to avoid noise?
2. Did certain thoughts or worries often cross your mind?
   How could you speak to these concerns in a new way
   in the coming weeks?
3. Did it help you deepen in solitude with God, or was it just
   inconvenient?

SATURDAY
ALMSGIVING:
CONSERVATION

The LORD is my shepherd, I shall not want.
He makes me lie down in green pastures;
he leads me beside still waters;
he restores my soul.
— Psalm 23:1–3a

The earth is the LORD's and all that is in it,
the world, and those who live in it.
— Psalm 24:1

Choose the form of almsgiving you will practice this week
or, if it gives you joy, do both. Give an amount that feels
generous and "hurts" a little in the context of your weekly
expenses. Grow in solitude by giving to others.

1. Give cash away to someone who asks you for it.
2. Mail a check or give online to a conservation organization. The greatest silence most of us will ever experience

is in the great outdoors; even the sounds of nature make a kind of silence, apart from the din of human noise. But human noise, development, and pollution are continually threatening to diminish the silence and well-being of our lands, waters, forests, wildlife habitats, and even deserts and mountainsides. Make a special Lenten gift to preserve silence, wilderness, and the good earth God has given us to:

— an environmental organization that focuses on the ecosystem of your town, county, or state
— a local, national, or international organization that works to protect or preserve what you consider your particular "spiritual geography" or a landscape that speaks to your heart and soul

Questions for Reflection

1. Does generosity make you feel rich or poor this week? Does it feel like a spiritual act?
2. How did you choose where to give your alms this week?
3. Did giving make more space within you for the presence of God? How?

WEEK TWO

SOLITUDE AND STRUGGLE

SUNDAY: ENDURING YOURSELF

Jacob was left alone; and a man wrestled with him until daybreak.

—Genesis 32:24

[Jesus] was in the wilderness forty days, tempted by Satan; and he was with the wild beasts; and the angels waited on him.

—Mark 1:13

One of the hardest things about practicing solitude as a spiritual discipline is learning to endure *yourself*. We are taught in Western culture to embrace and celebrate ourselves, but sometimes, like it or not, the self is a burden. Spending time in solitude is spending time with yourself, with no cushion or sweetener. Sometimes, that is blissful!

Sometimes, it is awkward and squirmy. Painful emotions we might normally try to suppress, like anger, fear, or grief, can surface in solitude, sometimes disguised as frustration, boredom, uncertainty, or sleepiness. All this can pull us away from solitude and the chance to go deeper with God.

We all have familiar—even comfortable—sins and weaknesses, which usually are papered over by distractions or indulged in order to get through the day. In solitude, they can come leaping to the forefront. Spending time alone can become entirely an exercise in self-endurance. It may mean becoming aware of the tricks and tendencies we have for avoiding pain, memories, or regrets we would rather forget but come knocking; or just the plain, old fact of the sinful self, boring and pathetic, presented before us without disguise or distraction. It can be quite uncomfortable, but if you can sit still and engage your discomfort, you can learn to endure your uncomfortable emotions. Fasting can help with this, too.

Consider the story of Jacob. He and his family were on a long journey and in the middle of a tense situation with his brother when he decided to spend a night alone with God. He sent his family and his servants across the river Jabbok, "and likewise everything that he had," and was left in solitude, without distractions or probably even a blanket. He didn't have a night of peaceful reverie; instead, God came in the form of a human man, not to console or direct him but to *wrestle* with him.

God and Jacob wrestled all night. Near dawn, God invited Jacob to give up: "Let me go, for the day is breaking." But Jacob couldn't stand to let God call it a draw: "I will not let you go, unless you bless me" (Gen. 32:26). So, God blessed Jacob and gave him a new name, but left him with a limp. Solitude is sure to lead you, too, to wrestling of one kind or another. Rather than avoiding it, use your Lenten discipline as an opportunity to practice it—and even to ask for a blessing.

Questions for Reflection

1. What struggles repeatedly surface for you in times of solitude or silence?
2. How might God be wrestling with you at this time in your life? What would it mean for you to say to God, "I will not let you go unless you bless me"?
3. Was it unfair for God to give Jacob a limp? What kind of "limp" might wrestling with God give you?

Choose a Practice for This Week

— Practice enduring yourself. If you haven't already tried a *poustinia* day, find a room where you can shut the door and stay there for at least two hours. Bring a notebook, a Bible, and some water, coffee, or tea to drink, but nothing else. Pray, reflect, read, write, or just stare out the window.

— Offer a confession of sin:
  • Make a half-hour appointment with a trusted pastor or a friend, or perhaps just with yourself.
  • Asking God to guide you to be both honest and gracious with yourself, write out in advance an unedited list of what you believe to be your sins: the ways you have wronged yourself, others, and God.
  • Bring that list to your appointment and read it aloud to the other person or to Jesus if you are alone. Consider using one of the two forms of "Reconciliation of a Penitent" in *The Book of Common Prayer* (pp. 447–52 or under "Pastoral Offices" at http://bcponline.org) with your pastor, priest, or yourself. Its words are unflinching but comforting.
  • If you do not use the *BCP*, read about God's assurance and grace in Psalm 103, Luke 7:36–50, or Romans 8:31–39.

MONDAY: ANTONY THE GREAT

The further the soul advances, the greater are the adversaries against which it must contend.

—Evagrius Ponticus[1]

You know the treachery of the demons; how fierce they are, yet how little power they have. Therefore do not fear them, but rather breathe Christ forever and trust Him.

—Antony the Great[2]

Antony was born in Egypt, two centuries after Jesus' death. His parents died when he was a young adult, and, as their oldest son, he inherited his family's wealth and property. Not long after, he heard and began to feel convicted by the teachings of Jesus on property and ownership, especially, "If you wish to be perfect, go, sell your possessions, and give the money to the poor, and you will have treasure in heaven; then come, follow me" (Matt. 19:21). He sold his family's land and possessions, found a place for his sister in a local convent (we don't have a record of what she thought of all this), and gave the money to the poor. Then, he went off on his own, seeking out other men who had given up everything and were living as hermits. Then, finally, he set out to the desert alone.

For the first twenty years, Antony lived in solitude in an abandoned fort, seeking God and battling the many demons who came to him until, as his biographer Athanasius says, "he came forth initiated in the mysteries and filled with the Spirit of God."[3] Other aspirants to hermit life were drawn to him and a community of hermits— known as a *laura*—gathered around him.

Antony is famous for his combat with demons and the Devil, who would regularly come and beat him to a pulp to punish him for trying to be so holy. They tried to lure him back to the comforts of his old life by plaguing his thoughts with "his wealth, care for his sister, claims of kindred, love of money, love of glory, the various pleasures of the table and the other relaxations of life, and at last the difficulty of virtue and the labor of it."⁴ Some of these things will sound familiar to us as reasons to avoid spiritual disciplines or even our deepest desires and dreams, things God may be calling us to do.

Whether you believe in the literal or metaphorical reality of demonic forces, solitude tends to attract them. They're also hard at work during the season of Lent. They come after us, trying to keep us from believing that prayer, good works, or self-discipline will amount to anything and reminding us of the comforts and pleasures we may be missing. "The Adversary" and "The Accuser" are ancient Hebrew names for the Devil for good reason; we moderns might add "The Critic" and "The Distracter," in light of more contemporary spiritual pitfalls.

Seeking the presence of God more deeply in silence and solitude will inevitably invite distractions, loss of heart, and a few demons into our lives. You may not get beaten to a pulp, as Antony did, but you will likely feel dejected, hopeless, bored, or sorry for yourself. You may sense the presence of the Evil One. The advice of Antony and other desert mothers and fathers was not to ignore demons or the Devil but to talk back to them. Like them, you might proclaim the name of Jesus or that "God is love." As a twenty-first-century Christian, you could also try: "I ain't gonna let nobody turn me around"⁵ and "Not today, Satan!"⁶ Don't let external or internal voices assault you without pushing back or making a snarky comeback. Like Antony, fight back and don't give up.

Questions for Reflection

1. What are the demonic voices that assault you most regularly or vigorously? They may try to shout you down in the form of setbacks, despair, boredom, distraction, numbing, procrastination, peer pressure, and so on. Make a list to help you identify them as they are happening in you and to resist them most effectively.
2. Would you feel silly telling a demonic voice to "back off" or "get out"? Or to actually say, whether aloud or in prayer, "Not today, Satan"? If so, what other ways of chasing away demons, critical voices, or dejection do you think could work for you?

TUESDAY: HAGAR OF EGYPT

The angel of the Lord *found her by a spring of water in the wilderness.*

—Genesis 16:7

Abraham rose early in the morning, and took bread and a skin of water, and gave it to Hagar, putting it on her shoulder, along with the child, and sent her away. And she departed, and wandered about in the wilderness of Beer-sheba.

—Genesis 21:14

Hagar is the first desert contemplative in the Judeo-Christian tradition. She left behind the human society of Abram and Sarai's camp and fled into the depths of the desert. There, she—a slave, a foreigner, and a concubine—encountered the living God. Now Hagar did not go into the desert looking for a mystical experience or even to do penance, like many of the desert mothers and fathers. Hagar just wanted to be free.

Hagar was the slave of Abram and Sarai, our beloved but flawed ancestors in faith. They were infertile, so Hagar was compelled to have a child with Abram on Sarai's behalf (it wouldn't be inaccurate to call this rape). However, becoming pregnant may have been that the first time Hagar felt her own power, because Genesis tells us it was then that she began to look "with contempt" on Sarai, her mistress. In response, Sarai "dealt harshly" with her, and so Hagar fled into the wilderness, pregnant and alone.

Sometimes we're forced into a time of wilderness or solitude, rather than choosing it of our own accord. It may be that we must endure long stretches of loneliness, suffering, or entrapment, but God doesn't desert us. The presence of God doesn't come to us only when we are free, at peace, or actively searching, but God is always seeking us, even when we're lost or in despair. God found Hagar in the wilderness and spoke to her.

She may have been angry or humiliated when the angel directed her to go back to Sarai (since it's not safe to be alone and pregnant in the desert). She had to give up her newfound freedom, but Hagar must have returned with a sense of specialness and worth. In her desert solitude, she met God, and she gave God a name: *El-roi,* or "God-who-sees" (Gen. 16:13). Her master and mistress couldn't see her as a full human being, but God did—and revealed the divine self to her, face-to-face.

Hagar endured her slavery for many years. She may have been comforted by watching her son, Ishmael, grow up and by her relationship with God, whom perhaps she continued to call *El Roi.* Her time of solitude in the wilderness may have given her the strength and hope to wait with hope and trust that God would provide for her. Abraham and Sarah finally banished Hagar after the birth of their own son, Isaac. She was rejected and in danger, but she was finally free. This time, God helped her settle down and survive. Hagar raised Ishmael to manhood in the wilderness and later arranged a marriage for him there. We never hear that she married. With freedom, solitude and the wilderness finally became her home.

Questions for Reflection

1. Has solitude ever helped you through a time of confinement or oppression? Was your solitude forced or chosen? How did it help you?
2. Feeling seen and loved by God is not something we need to earn or wait for. Does Hagar's story give you hope, if you are in a time of struggle or exile?
3. Have you felt beheld or specially seen by God in your times of solitude? If not, consider praying and asking God to be present to you in that way.

WEDNESDAY: SAUL AT DAMASCUS

Saul got up from the ground, and though his eyes were open, he could see nothing; so they led him by the hand and brought him into Damascus. For three days he was without sight, and neither ate nor drank.

—Acts 9:8–9

Last of all, as to one untimely born, he appeared also to me. For I am the least of the apostles, unfit to be called an apostle, because I persecuted the church of God. But by the grace of God I am what I am, and his grace toward me has not been in vain. On the contrary, I worked harder than any of them — though it was not I, but the grace of God that is with me.

—1 Corinthians 15:8–10

Saul lived an intense and active life in the years before he met Jesus on the road to Damascus. He traveled all around Israel, persecuting and arresting Christians, witnessing at least a few executions,[7] and working constantly to track down new suspects. He was an educated Roman citizen, committed to civil order and the life of the mind; a Jew, part of a respected and a persecuted minority; and a Pharisee, committed to living according to the law of his people. He was disciplined, driven, and zealous. After his conversion experience, he would again live a tremendously active life, traveling to Arabia, Syria, and all over the Mediterranean. However, after he fell off that horse, Saul, who was probably what we would now call an extrovert, went into seclusion. Blinded and in shock, his friends "led him by the hand" to a safe place where he could recover, in solitude.

Perhaps the Lord knew that the only way Saul would stand still long enough to consider his life and call was if he was struck completely blind. He *had* to stay indoors and be waited on by others; he couldn't travel, read, or write. He couldn't distract himself or avoid what God was trying to say to him. The words Jesus had said to him, in fact, must have been ringing in his ears: "Saul, Saul, why do you persecute me?" (Acts 9:4). He had nothing to do but sit and listen: to Jesus' words, to his guilt, to God's grace, and for what Jesus might say next.

We can keep ourselves busy and distracted enough to drown out what God is trying to say to us, whether unconsciously or purposely. We can't special-order a blinding conversion experience, but we can choose times and places to "get stuck" so that we have to listen and focus on Christ and ourselves. It's not easy to get away for a three-day retreat—even Saul had to be forced to do it—but it's not impossible. Perhaps in your Lenten calendar planning, you have scheduled a daylong or weekend retreat. If not, don't underestimate the effectiveness of even a few hours or even *one* hour. Choosing to spend time alone, with little stimulation or distraction, can reveal things of Christ and his guidance to us that we otherwise don't hear or see.

It may be that, like Saul, we'll be confronted in solitude with our own guilt and sin or with some other powerful feeling or realization we've been suppressing. To assure Saul of God's grace, Jesus sent a man named Ananias to find him in his solitude and to bring him a good word. It may be that Jesus sends someone to you too. Or, since unlike Saul, you are *planning* to spend some time apart, you may want to arrange for a subsequent conversation with a pastor or close friend, especially if you're an extrovert, or process your feelings by talking about them.

Spending time apart gives us space and time to try to sit in the presence of God, even if it makes us squirm. We can notice our feelings, listen for Jesus' voice, do some discernment, and simply seek to know Jesus better by offering ourselves, without distraction and as we are, to his voice, grace, and love.

Questions for Reflection

1. Have you ever taken a "time-out" in your life, like Saul did? What was it like? Was it a struggle, or was it peaceful? Did you have a helper like Ananias?
2. Paul confronted his sin and shame, first alone with God and then probably sharing it also with Ananias. Later, he often freely spoke of his past sins and regrets, sharing them with his congregations. How hard would it be to share some of your shame or past sins with others? With a special person or mentor like Ananias? Could it be redemptive for you to share your past sins or regrets as freely and publicly as Paul did?

# THURSDAY:
FRANCIS OF ASSISI

*Then Jesus told his disciples, "If any want to become my
followers, let them deny themselves and take up their cross
and follow me."*

—Matthew 16:24

*The Friars should appropriate to themselves nothing,
neither house, nor place, nor anything at all; but as pilgrims
and strangers in this world, serving the Lord in poverty and
humility, they should go seeking alms with confidence. Nor
ought they be ashamed, since for our sakes, our Lord made
Himself poor in this world.*

—*Rule of 1223 of Saint Francis of Assisi*

Francis lived a joyful but physically painful life. He and his
followers begged for scraps of food and slept where they
could. They walked barefoot, wearing rags, often singing.
He loved the open road and rough traveling as a form of
penance and solidarity with the poor, but over time, this
way of life would weaken and erode his body terribly. He
developed a painful eye condition, his stomach troubled
him constantly, and his stigmata bled, oozed, and ached.

Even still, Francis carried his solitude with him into the
crowds of people he encountered. He was deeply convicted
in his call from God: to give away all he had, to live in solidarity with the poor and sick, and to find joy in God alone.
However, his deepest pain may have been his anguish at
choosing between a life of solitude and contemplation and
a life of active preaching and ministry to the poor and sick.
Although Francis lived his life almost constantly on the
road—throughout his native Umbria and to Rome, Spain,

Egypt, and the Holy Land—he also loved quiet places like caves, his church at San Damiano, and the forest chapel that came to be called La Portiuncula ("the little portion"), where he lived with his brothers on and off until the end of his life.

There was a place inside Francis always set aside for the pure contemplation of the presence of God. It was as if he carried a chapel within him, which after times of extreme exertion or emotion needed restoring in solitude with God. Others realized this about Francis's well-being; his brothers would often remove him to a hermitage, a friendly monastery, or back to La Portiuncula to rest. Early in Francis's ministry, a rich donor gave him the mountain of La Verna, a quiet place where he could get away and where later he would receive the stigmata.

Francis's most intimate moments of solitude with God seemed also to have been marked by pain, as epitomized by his stigmata. Late in his life, Francis prayed to be unified with Christ in his suffering of the Passion and Crucifixion. Some people don't believe that Francis actually and literally received the wounds of Christ, but Francis believed that he did. He carried these wounds in the solitude of himself, always keeping them carefully wrapped and hidden away from view. Strangely for us, perhaps, they were the most intimate and powerful experience he had of God's love and grace.

For Francis, a life of painful struggle was the truest way to live life close to Christ. I admit I have trouble understanding this. I do, however, understand his vacillations between a life of solitude and a life among people; I love both, too. I'm inspired by his embrace of rough living as a penance and portal to Christ and as a way to live in solidarity with the poor. Looking to Francis, whose joy and love went so deep, I find courage for solitude, even through struggle and pain, in my Lenten discipline and in my life.

Questions for Reflection

1. How would you describe your tolerance for pain? Is there a difference for you in facing pain if you know there is a tangible reward—for instance, in vigorous exercise, getting a tattoo, or staying up all night to finish a project—and if there is not—for instance, in fasting?
2. Do you have a hard time choosing between contemplation in solitude or serving and being in the company of others?
3. Is there a relationship between pain and solitude in your spiritual life? How would you characterize it? Does Francis inspire or concern you, as you consider his and your relationship to pain? Why?

 FRIDAY FASTING: NO PAIN, NO GAIN?

Skip Lunch to Pray

I [King David] will not offer burnt offerings to the LORD my God that cost me nothing.

—2 Samuel 24:24

I appeal to you therefore, brothers and sisters, by the mercies of God, to present your bodies as a living sacrifice, holy and acceptable to God, which is your spiritual worship.

—Romans 12:1

Inspiration

In Lent, we engage with the dangerous proposition that self-denial is beneficial. This can be taken to extremes, but the most effective spiritual practices should be somewhat of a struggle. In the words of so many coaches and personal trainers: "No pain, no gain." We are better at doing this for our bodies through exercise routines or special diets than we are at stretching and exercising our relationship with Jesus.

Fasting is not easy, but giving up a day or more of meals as a form of prayer has been a rewarding discipline for Christians for centuries. Since so many of the solitaries and faithful people featured in this book practiced it and praised it, I want to offer ways for beginners to follow in their footsteps, not just to feel tough but as a way to grow closer to God. For more thoughts and instructions about fasting from a meal, see the "Preparing for Lent" chapter at the beginning of this book.

Practice

Skip lunch. Go somewhere you can spend the time and energy you would on lunch to talk to Jesus or to spend time in prayer whether by sitting, or walking, or reading the Bible or another spiritual book. *If there is any reason fasting from food may not be good for your health, repeat a past Friday fast or do not fast at all.*

Do not snack, or overload at the previous meal. If you feel hungry, sip hot tea or warm water. Breathe into the hunger, ask for the presence of the Holy Spirit, and engage or offer difficult feelings or pains in prayer to Jesus; "offer it up," as they say. If at all possible, do not announce or reveal your fast to others outside your immediate family, if even them. If skipping lunch would be too noticeable, skip dinner or breakfast instead.

Questions for Reflection

1. What feelings arose because of your fast today? Fatigue? Grumpiness? Helplessness? Were you able to engage those feelings through prayer, or was it hard to disconnect from them?
2. What do you think about the idea that spirituality "costs" something? In what ways might a close relationship with God or a mature prayer life require sacrifice or come at a cost to other priorities or comforts in your life?
3. Did fasting help you deepen in solitude with God, or was it just inconvenient?

SATURDAY ALMSGIVING: ILLNESS

I was sick and you took care of me.
— Matthew 25:36c

Then Jesus called the twelve together and gave them power and authority over all demons and to cure diseases.
— Luke 9:1

Choose the form of almsgiving you will practice this week or, if it gives you joy, do both. Give an amount that feels generous and "hurts" a little in the context of your weekly expenses. Grow in solitude by giving to others.

1. Give cash away to someone who asks you for it.
2. Mail a check or give online to a hospital or health organization. People facing a major illness—like cancer,

AIDS, multiple sclerosis, or schizophrenia—often endure deeply difficult spiritual struggles in the midst of terrible physical and emotional suffering. Illness forces some to face the limits of their bodies and wills in much the way Christians choose to do when we fast or do penance. However, those who are well have a choice of when to start and stop, which those who are sick do not. Make a special Lenten gift to support those who are forced to struggle with their bodies, brains, or endurance because of disease, disability, or injury:

— a local hospital or hospice organization, especially one that has helped you or someone you care about
— a local organization that helps underserved populations get mental health treatment
— an organization funding research for the treatment and cure of a condition or disease that you or someone you loved has faced

Questions for Reflection

1. Does generosity make you feel rich or poor this week? Does it feel like a spiritual act?
2. How did you choose where to give your alms this week?
3. Did giving make more space within you for the presence of God? How?

WEEK THREE

SOLITUDE AND JOURNEYS

SUNDAY:
TAKING A WALK

He said to them, "Come away to a deserted place all by yourselves and rest a while." For many were coming and going, and they had no leisure even to eat. And they went away in the boat to a deserted place by themselves.
—Mark 6:31–32

Solvitur ambulando — *"It is solved by walking."*
—Saint Augustine of Hippo[1]

As powerful as it can be to stay put in a *poustinia* for a whole day or to sit *zazen* in a Zen center, walking and pilgrimage have long been used in the Christian tradition as engines for prayer and meditation. Most monasteries have cloisters (enclosed walkways) and grounds so that members can take walks, inside or outside, whatever the weather. The ancient practice of pilgrimage means to go on a journey, not to relax or see the sights but to better see God and ourselves. As writer and blogger Vinita Hampton Wright puts it, "We learn God's will by moving toward something—whatever seems right to us. In the way that you cannot steer a parked car, God cannot direct us while we are sitting rigidly in our fear and over-caution."[2] Engaging in solitude by traveling away from your ordinary life is a spiritual practice with ancient biblical precedent, from Abram, Sarai, and Hagar leaving home, to Elijah on Mount Horeb, to Jesus going into the desert for forty days and forty nights.

Pilgrimage gets us out of our ordinary places to experience God and ourselves in new ways. We go outward in order to go inward. John Muir wrote, "I only went out for a walk and finally concluded to stay out till sundown, for going out, I found, was really going in."[3] Some people travel the world on pilgrimage, but you can also take a long walk, take a train across town, or take a boat or ferry ride, just like Jesus and the disciples.

A pilgrimage journey of any kind gives the soul permission to wander and explore alongside the body. You can let go into time and space as a bus, train, boat, or plane takes you somewhere else, knowing you're accomplishing a task even while you look out the window. On a bike or on foot, when we need to concentrate more on our mode of travel, our hearts and souls still can follow our bodies to wander and explore in wonder and prayer-in-motion. Traveling is a way of both paying closer attention and not paying much attention at all (just be careful crossing the street).

Sometimes, on stressful days in my work as a parish priest, I would walk in circles around my church sanctuary, talking to God and letting the movement of my body calm me down. Even without a destination, you can make a journey, letting go into the movement of your body, even if it's just around a room you know well. It can change your thinking as well as your heart rate, and it can help you get deeper into prayer and meditation with God.

Questions for Reflection

1. Notice how moving, walking, or traveling changes the way your brain works. What else do you notice about your heartbeat, your mood, or your anxiety levels when you're in movement?
2. What are some reasons that it may be hard to step out of your ordinary life or geography to go for a walk or on a journey? How can you overcome or work around those impediments, even just for this week?

Choose a Practice for This Week

— Take a journey in solitude by going on a long walk by yourself. If you can, take a walk in some real wilderness! If it's too hot, too cold, or unsafe where you are to walk outdoors, take a walk indoors instead — at a mall, a gym, your church, or even up and down a hallway. If it's cold in your part of the world, you can bundle up and pray, "Bless the Lord, ice and cold, / . . . Bless the Lord, frosts and snows."[4]

— Take a journey in solitude by getting on a form of public transportation in your area and riding to a remote station and back, or perhaps even up and down an entire route. (I don't recommend making your journey by car because then you really should focus on driving.) Look out the window, ruminate, silently pray the office of Morning or Evening Prayer according to your tradition, read a book on pilgrimage or the book of Jonah, or daydream about a more dramatic pilgrimage trip you would like to take.

MONDAY: JESUS LEFT THE CROWDS

And after he had dismissed the crowds, he went up the mountain by himself to pray. When evening came, he was there alone.

—Matthew 14:23

But he would withdraw to deserted places and pray.

—Luke 5:16

Jesus and his disciples were busy: constantly on the move, sought out by the curious and by people in need, responding to the confrontations of Pharisees and other detractors, healing, and preaching. Jesus often tried to get away, sometimes bringing his disciples with him. However, his attempts to withdraw were almost always foiled; the disciples came looking for him, the crowds figured out where he had gone and followed, or the disciples got themselves caught in a storm and he had to walk out across the sea to save them. I imagine Jesus as a parent who couldn't even use the bathroom without the kids banging on the door—"Mom? Where are you?" Still, he kept trying, going up on mountains and to many other "deserted places" to pray and be still. Interestingly, he seemed always to choose a place outdoors.

I wonder if it was a relief for Jesus to walk away from the usual places of his ministry—as Thoreau once wrote, "to shake off the village"[5]—and physically be someplace else. He would leave Galilee for Gentile towns or head into Samaria. He would get into a boat with his disciples and sail out to the middle of the lake. (Even then, the Gospels recount that people would call out to him from shore.) Similarly, individuals and church groups find it helpful to go away for retreats, away from their usual environments. Sometimes people do better work in a coffee shop or library than at the office or at home. Prayer also can happen more easily and effectively for some people in places that are outside the normal geography of their lives.

If you track him through the Gospels, you can see that Jesus went off alone most often after times of great exertion or emotional distress. For instance, after he learned of the execution of John the Baptist, after feeding the five thousand, after extreme acts of healing or exorcizing of demons, and finally, the night before his arrest and crucifixion. Jesus even took walks after his resurrection, first with two people on the road to Emmaus and then with his disciples to Bethany, before his ascension (Luke 24:13–28, 50).

Walking can be a stress reliever but why not also an impetus to prayer? Get out of some of your usual spaces and take a walk to any place not part of your daily routine, maybe even somewhere you've never been before. There are many ways to get away from your ordinary geography—even in indoor spaces—like malls, airports, or museums. You may be able to hear God's voice away from "the village" in a way you can't in the midst of the crowds and byways of your everyday life.

Questions for Reflection

1. How easy it is for you to "leave the crowds" or busyness of your ordinary life? Do you do it much?
2. What would it look like for you to feel you have "shaken off the village" in your own life?
3. Do you find it easier or harder to pray while you're on a walk?

TUESDAY: THE CORACLE MONKS

Jesus was led up by the Spirit into the wilderness.
—Matthew 4:1a

> *Christ be with me, Christ within me,*
> *Christ behind me, Christ before me,*
> *Christ beside me, Christ to win me,*
> *Christ to comfort and restore me,*
> *Christ beneath me, Christ above me,*
> *Christ in quiet, Christ in danger,*
> *Christ in hearts of all that love me,*
> *Christ in mouth of friend and stranger.*
> —Saint Patrick's "Breastplate,"
> a traditional Irish blessing

The earliest monks of Christian Ireland and Britain weren't in search of peaceful solitude when they sailed away from their homes and towns to seek a monastic life across the sea. Suffering in solitude was considered the way to follow Christ in Celtic monasticism, in what came to be known as a "blue" martyrdom. Untold numbers of young men (and probably at least a few women) ventured out in small wood-and-leather boats called coracles, usually without a sail or paddles, to totally throw themselves into the hands of God's mercy and guidance. The hope was that God would beach their boat in a place they could build a monastery or hermitage. There, they would live out their lives in solitude, prayer, and penance. This was called a blue (or green) martyrdom, not only because of the blue-green of the sea but also because, as the popular explanation goes, in Gaelic *glas* means "blue-gray-green," which is the color the monks were said to turn from so much hardship and fasting!

There must have been a thrill in the uncertainty and adventure of those journeys, despite the danger, for these aspiring adventurer-penitents. There is an account of three monks whose coracle beached along the English coast and subsequently appeared before King Alfred the Great. When he asked why they had come, they said, "We stole away because we wanted for the love of God to be on pilgrimage, and we cared not where."

George McLeod, also a Celtic Christian and founder of the renowned Iona Community of Scotland, once said, "Christians are explorers, not map makers."[6] Many Christians find great joy in heading off on mission trips, pilgrimage, or "holy hikes." Still, most of us would hesitate to set out without a compass, paddles, or GPS. Still, we hunger, if not literally to get lost in God's creation, to more figuratively get lost in its beauty: hiking through wilderness or sailing on open water, sitting under a tree or on a back porch, gazing at a sunrise or a starry sky. Losing ourselves in God's world—especially in solitude—is a way of losing ourselves in God's presence.

Walking a labyrinth can also be a way to lose yourself. By walking a winding path, round and round until you reach the center, you travel without worrying about where you're going, just that you're on the journey and in God's presence. A labyrinth lets you go on a meandering adventure or pilgrimage without having to travel far or spend any money, the same reasons they were used by medieval Christians at cathedrals like Chartres, an easier pilgrimage for many than trekking to Rome or Jerusalem.

This week, try taking a walk without a clear destination in mind—in your neighborhood, in a natural setting, or in a labyrinth—letting the Holy Spirit nudge you along the path. Opening yourself physically to God's leading, even just down the sidewalk, may open you to God's leading in other parts of your life. Remember the Celtic hermits in their little boats and their outrageous — even foolhardy — faith that God would go with them.

Questions for Reflection

1. What are some journeys or adventures you have enjoyed in your life? How did solitude play a part, if at all?
2. In what ways could you use your prayer time for exploring and taking risks?
3. You might open yourself to discovering a new place to walk or stroll along your usual routes just by happenstance rather than making a plan, like the coracle monks. You might be surprised by the paths, parks, or walkways you find in places you thought you knew well. Does the Holy Spirit have something new to say to you in what you find or see?

WEDNESDAY: MARY OF EGYPT

Therefore, I will now allure her,
and bring her into the wilderness,
and speak tenderly to her.
— Hosea 2:14

If you cross the Jordan, you will find glorious rest.
— A voice heard by Mary of Egypt

Mary was a fun-loving, bed-hopping, independent woman living in fourth-century Alexandria, Egypt. From the age of twelve, she had made her living spinning flax, begging, and currying favors from men. When she was about twenty-nine, thinking she would meet lovers and have some fun, she joined a pilgrimage group traveling to Jerusalem for the feast of the Holy Cross (September 14). Upon arriving, however, she found herself irrepressibly drawn to the Church of the Holy Sepulchre. Three times she felt physically thwarted from crossing over the church's threshold. Then she saw an image of the Virgin Mary in the front portico and asked her for help, promising to change her life and to go wherever the mother of God might send her if she could be allowed to enter the church.

She was then able to enter that most holy place. When she saw the relics of the cross displayed for the feast, she was overwhelmed by feelings of God's love and grace. She then returned to the Virgin in the portico and offered herself once again. She heard the words, "If you cross the Jordan you will find glorious rest." So Mary went down from Jerusalem to the Jordan valley and found a monastery, where she baptized herself in the river and received the Eucharist for the first time. The next day, she crossed over alone into the great desert on the other side, more independent than she had ever been in Alexandria and yet completely dependent on God. She lived there many years, growing old, burned and bleached by the sun, until she was discovered by a monk named Zosimas. She died soon after and legend says that a lion—an ancient symbol for Christ—helped Zosimas bury her in the sand.

Mary wandered the Jordanian desert alone for decades. It was a difficult life, she told Zosimas; she was always too hot or too cold, she missed the food and wine she had known in Alexandria, and she was lonely. But in the desert, she found true love. In the city she had known the thrill of sex, but it was with God and Mary, the *Theotokos*, that she felt known, cherished, and at peace. As a woman who had long lived by her own wits and means, living alone in the wilderness must have suited her better than life in a convent.

Like Mary of Egypt, consider using walking and wandering as a time for meditative confession. Walking your confession can keep your heart and mind from getting stuck in shame or overthinking. As you offer your sins, regrets, and weaknesses to God, believe that God will "speak tenderly" to you and cherish you. Solitude helped Mary purge feelings of shame and regret, but only because she had such trust in the care of Mary at her side and of her savior, Jesus Christ.

Questions for Reflection

1. Do you make a regular practice of reflecting on your sins and weaknesses? Would you like to do so, if you don't? Why or why not?
2. How do you find and feel assurance of God's forgiveness and absolution? Is this easier for you in community or in solitude?
3. How might you "walk out" your confession like Mary of Egypt, whether in the desert or just up and down your hallway?

THURSDAY: JONAH RUNS AWAY

"You cast me into the deep,
*   into the heart of the seas,*
*   and the flood surrounded me;*
all your waves and your billows
*   passed over me.*
Then I said, 'I am driven away
*   from your sight;*
how shall I look again
*   upon your holy temple?'*
The waters closed in over me;

the deep surrounded me;
weeds were wrapped around my head
     at the roots of the mountains.
I went down to the land
     whose bars closed upon me forever;
yet you brought up my life from the Pit,
     O LORD my God."
                                   —Jonah 2:3–6

"Be still, and know that I am God!"
                          —Psalm 46:10

Jonah the prophet went on a journey that he did not plan
to take—twice. When God asked him to go to Nineveh,
instead of traveling east across the desert toward that city
and without saying so much as a word to God in response,
Jonah got on a boat sailing west for Tarshish, heading as far
in the other direction as possible. God sent a terrible storm
to get him turned around in the right direction. Knowing
who God was after and trying to save his shipmates, Jonah
jumped overboard. Mercifully, God provided a big fish to
swallow him up: both to save his life and to give him some
time to "think about his choices," as my mother used to say.
Sealed in the cloister of a fish belly and deep under the sea,
Jonah was finally willing to begin a conversation with God.

There are journeys in life we don't want to take and
places we don't want to go. There are things God may be
calling us to do that we feel unable to undertake. Sometimes we just ignore the situation, and sometimes we run
as far in the other direction as we possibly can. The story
of Jonah is a parable and hyperbole about what happens
when we try to run from God and about the bitter fruits of
self-righteous pride.

Neither Jonah's travels nor his solitude were freely chosen. Like Jonah, we're not likely to feel rested or protected
so much as *stuck* in this kind of solitude. The dark, damp,

stinky confinement of a fish belly might not be far off from experiences you have had in your own life. Sometimes solitude is painful or suffocating, and sometimes it's forced on us, even if the circumstances that brought us there are of our own making.

Jonah's prayer from the fish belly is a lament but also a thanksgiving for his safety. This is also the first time he has spoken to God in the whole story. I don't like to think that God backs us into corners to get us to pray or acknowledge a call, but throughout the arc of the Bible the Spirit goes to great lengths (and depths) to bring human beings into relationship. As an unlooked-for bonus, the hardships and suffering of men and women in the Bible teach them greater compassion, humility, and integrity, too. (Not Jonah, though; see 4:1–11.)

Getting stuck in a time and place of solitude is not as inspiring as choosing it of our own free will, but enforced solitude can still push us to pray or to speak with God when otherwise we may just want to turn away. It can make us face ourselves, the consequences of our choices, and where the Spirit may be trying to draw us. If nothing else, it can also give us a place to lament and cry out for help, trusting that God will not abandon us even when it seems that all is lost.

Questions for Reflection

1. When have you been alone on a journey that you didn't choose? What were the circumstances?
2. Has a time of solitude helped in a time of discernment or decision making in your own life? Was that solitude forced on you or chosen?
3. How easy is it for you to take some time to talk to God about what is happening in your life, how you feel about it, or what God is asking you to do? Does it ever seem like God is trying to chase you down, to get you to stop and listen?

 FRIDAY FASTING: BOREDOM

Fast from Social Media, Games, and Online Diversions

Fasting is wonderful, because it tramples our sins like a dirty weed, while it cultivates and raises truth like a flower.
— John Chrysostom[7]

Inspiration

Most of us live an everyday life that's extremely full — of food, drinks, activity, noise, entertainment, choices, and distractions. There's a lot to distract us from the stress, pain, or emotions we may be feeling, at least some of which may be trying to get our attention to change something about our lives or our relationships with God. There's a lot to distract us from the people we love, the poor, social injustice, and the work and tasks that we need to do every day. Perhaps we need some boredom *sometimes*?

Choosing to fast is choosing to "enter into emptiness," as Brother Aiden Owen, a brother of the Order of the Holy Cross, puts it in a blog series on fasting.[8] Fasting, whatever form it takes, helps us resist the too-fullness, the crazy busyness, and the comforting numbness that we often fall into in human life. The emptiness makes more room for solitude but also for anxiety. Brother Aiden writes, "When faced with this anxiety most of us are tempted to throw in the towel and eat something or drink something or check our e-mail yet again. The solution to this anxiety, though, is to move deeper into it . . . emptiness hollows us out and wakes us up. Entering into emptiness is a way of creating space for an encounter with God and offering God the opportunity to fill us with what we need, which ultimately is to be filled with God's own self."[9]

Practice

Fast from entertainment and news today: online, in books, on television, on your phone, or elsewhere. Try not to look up information you need online; look elsewhere or go without. Choose quiet and solitude instead. For a different form of distraction, go for a walk, clean up a mess, talk to a friend or a child, or pray for people and places in your life that need God's love and healing.

If at all possible, do not announce or reveal your fast to others outside your immediate family, if even them. If you want, keep your fast for the whole weekend. If you're feeling the need for an even greater challenge, keep this fast until next Friday.

Questions for Reflection

1. Did you feel a bloom of "truth, like a flower" from your fast today? What truth bloomed? Or what "weeds" do you feel you were able to trample?
2. What did you notice about the role of entertainment and diversion in your daily life?
3. Did it help you deepen in solitude with God, or was it just inconvenient?

SATURDAY ALMSGIVING: REFUGEES

Do not neglect to show hospitality to strangers, for by doing that some have entertained angels without knowing it.
—Hebrews 13:2

The alien who resides with you shall be to you as the citizen among you; you shall love the alien as yourself, for you were aliens in the land of Egypt: I am the LORD your God.
—Leviticus 19:34

Choose the form of almsgiving you will practice this week or, if it gives you joy, do both. Give an amount that feels generous and "hurts" a little in the context of your weekly expenses. Grow in solitude by giving to others.

1. Give cash away to someone who asks you for it.
2. Mail a check or give online to a refugee organization. Refugees are forced to go on journeys they do not choose, to leave home, escape persecution or violence, often with little but the clothes on their backs. We live in a time when there are more refugees at large than since the years immediately following World War II. Many people have become strangers in a strange land. Make a Lenten gift of alms to help refugees make a safe and peaceful journey to a new home:
   — an organization that helps refugees settle and make a home in your area
   — an international aid organization for refugees at their point of escape or in refugee camps

Questions for Reflection

1. Does generosity make you feel rich or poor this week? Does it feel like a spiritual act?
2. How did you choose where to give your alms this week?
3. Did giving make more space within you for the presence of God? How?

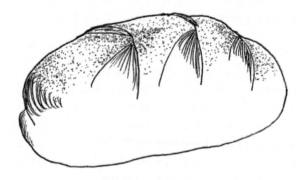

WEEK FOUR

SOLITUDE AND
HOSPITALITY

SUNDAY:
WELCOMING
GUESTS

I was a stranger and you welcomed me.
—Matthew 25:35c

A woman named Martha welcomed [Jesus] into her home.
She had a sister named Mary, who sat at the Lord's feet and
listened to what he was saying. But Martha was distracted
by her many tasks.

—Luke 10:38–40

Hospitality and solitude keep each other in balance. The
saints and rebels we know best as solitaries or hermits made
hospitality to guests and neighbors a part of that practice:
Antony the Great, Julian of Norwich, Seraphim of Sarov,
Charles de Foucauld, and Thomas Merton. Others spent

part of their lives in solitude and then became radically active in public life: Martin of Tours, Benedict of Nursia, Francis of Assisi, and Catherine of Siena. Solitude in the Christian tradition is a path through the self that leads to God and Jesus but also to our neighbor.

The story of Mary and Martha is a parable about solitude and hospitality. When Jesus came to their home, Martha kept busy while Mary sat with him, listening to him. Certainly, guests appreciate a hot meal and a clean house, but Martha didn't ever come sit down and talk with her guest—a guest who wouldn't be around long, or not like this.

My husband and I live with three furry animals, two litter boxes, clothing that seems to migrate to every corner of the house, as well as scattered books, cups, papers, dog toys, and shoes. I find entertaining a burden because cleaning up the mess feels so overwhelming. Yet, when friends and family do visit, I remember that they're simply glad to be in our home—our most sacred space—to talk, to watch a movie, to share a meal. Most friends care less about dust bunnies, clutter, or perfect dinners and more about being together. Jesus told Martha the very same thing: "Martha, Martha, you are worried and distracted by many things; there is need of only one thing. Mary has chosen the better part, which will not be taken away from her" (Luke 10:41–42).

Catherine Doherty wrote that when anyone enters a *poustinia*, "the whole of humanity enters into that cabin with them."[1] In her homeland of Russia, she explains, a lifetime spent in a *poustinia* was considered a ministry to the local community through prayer, penance, and offering of the self to whomever might stop by to ask for prayer, counsel, help in the hay fields, or a bite to eat.

Making room for God within ourselves means that there is more room for others, too, in our homes, in our prayers, in our work, and in our hearts.

Questions for Reflection

1. How have you seen the balance (or imbalance) of solitude and hospitality at work in your own life lately?
2. How could you think about "the whole of humanity" entering into your times of solitude or *poustinia* with you? Doherty also wrote, "It was for all mankind that the poustinik was to pray, to weep, and to endure all the temptations that come to him who lives in the desert."[2] We live in a culture that focuses on the spirituality of the individual; what it is like to think about your spirituality as a part of the spirituality of your community, your city, or your nation? Or even "the whole of humanity"?!

Choose a Practice for This Week

— Make a pot of soup or a loaf of bread (see appendix B for "Easy Little Bread") for someone who needs it. Cook in solitude, if you can, and without any radio or music; talk aloud or in your head to God about the person you're cooking for, offering your work as an act of love and prayer.
— Go sit in solitude in an otherwise crowded place. Places you might try: café, transit station, government building, hospital. Or kick it up a notch and go sit in places few people go unless they have to (where you may have to pray from your car or across the street): nursing home, currency exchange, juvenile detention center, prison.
— Watch and pray for the people who go by or who are sitting around you.
— Let the crowd inspire you to pray for the whole of humanity, sending God's love out to meet its needs and pains as well as its sins and need for repentance.

MONDAY:
BENEDICT
OF NURSIA

Let all guests who arrive be received like Christ.
—Rule of Saint Benedict

As soon as anyone knocks, or a poor man calls out, the porter replies, "Thanks be to God" or "Your blessing, please"; then with all the gentleness that comes from the fear of God, he provides a prompt answer with the warmth of love.
—Rule of Saint Benedict

When he was a young man, Benedict moved from the little mountain town where he grew up to get an education in the very big city of Rome. Benedict hated Rome. When he left, instead of returning to his family in Nursia, he headed for Subiaco, another mountain town that was a bit closer and where he was not a hometown kid. His biographer, urbanite Pope Gregory the Great, who lived in Rome or Constantinople his whole life, declared it "a lonely wilderness."[3] Benedict found a suitable cave in the mountains above town and lived there as a hermit for three years, seeking God through fasting, praying, and penance.

If Benedict was hoping for complete solitude, he didn't get it. Not long after he settled into his cave, local shepherds discovered him. Benedict must have felt compassion for them because instead of telling them to go away, tradition says that he taught and prayed with them. The lowest room of his series of caves, which you can still visit at Subiaco, is named "The Shepherd's Cave" for this, his first act of hospitality.

If he had been a grump, he would've been left alone, but he wasn't and before long, word spread from the shepherds, to the townspeople, then all over the region, that a wise and holy man was living among them. People began to visit Benedict for counsel, and some men asked to join him in his religious life. A monastic community formed around him, and it wasn't long before there were twelve small communities across the mountains, all overseen by Benedict. (One community later tried to poison him, but that's another story.)

Many years went by before Benedict wrote his famous *Regula* or Rule: instruction and inspiration for the purpose, prayer life, etiquette, and governing structure of living in monastic community. The primary work of a monastic community is the daily office—to pray for the world; however, Benedict made hospitality a close second. He gave instructions for hospitality in details large and small, from the command to welcome all guests as though they were Christ himself, to the joyful greeting a porter should give each visitor, to the directive that guests should eat at the abbot's table and that "adequate bedding" be available in the guest quarters—nothing luxurious but no scrimping.

As you sit in crowded places this week, remember Benedict and the shepherds who came to his door. The purpose of solitude is to encounter God *and* to grow in compassion and hospitality for others. These two must stay in balance. In his monasteries, Benedict tried to strike that balance by assigning separate sleeping quarters to guests and monks and even by forbidding monks from initiating conversations with guests without permission. We may not be so strict in our own lives, but as our relationship with God feeds and broadens our hospitality and compassion, we still need a life of prayer and some solitude to feed our souls. Otherwise we may be hard-pressed to truly give of ourselves, instead of just putting on a happy face, grudgingly doing our duty, or indulging a self-righteous belief that we can fix or help all whom we encounter.

Benedict presented hospitality as both a spiritual discipline and an ongoing spiritual wellness test for religious communities. It can serve as a similar check for individuals, families, small groups, and congregations: is our life of faith and prayer bearing fruit of the Spirit or not? Do we welcome strangers and visitors into our midst with compassion and joy? Or do we resist and distance ourselves from them? The fruit of Christian solitude is genuine hospitality.

Questions for Reflection

1. Is showing hospitality to others easy or hard for you, or somewhere in between? What circumstances make it easiest for you to offer hospitality? What makes it harder?
2. Are your levels of hospitality and solitude in balance right now? (Those levels may or may not be 50/50.) How can you tell? If not, what are some ways could you get them more in balance?

TUESDAY: JULIAN OF NORWICH

Know it well: love was his meaning.
—Julian of Norwich,
Revelations of Divine Love

There is no fear in love, but perfect love drives out fear, because fear expects punishment. The person who is afraid has not been made perfect in love. We love because God first loved us. If anyone says, I love God, and hates a brother or sister, he is a liar, because the person who doesn't love a brother or sister who can be seen can't love God, who can't be seen.
—1 John 4:18–20 (CEB)

Julian chose the life of an anchoress: to live out her days locked in a little house built alongside a parish church. It may sound like a prison, but she had windows, a servant for her domestic needs, and a cat to keep down the mice. For a woman of the fourteenth century, it was a miraculous blessing to have "a room of her own" with quiet and time to think, pray, and, eventually, to write.

Instead of a lonely desert or a forest, Julian's cell was set in the middle of a busy port city, with all its crowds, noises, and odors. Her solitude wasn't for just herself, but a gift to a whole, chaotic city. Anyone who walked by would know that she was praying for them and all their neighbors and that they could go to her for counsel or a word from God. One of her windows was expressly for this purpose, looking out onto a little porch where any-one could come to sit and speak with her, albeit through a black curtain.[4] In return, people of her city brought her food and other gifts.

The temptation for someone chosen to be sealed in a house-sized tabernacle could be self-righteous instructive-ness and pride or, alternately, aloof smugness and self-protection. It is easy to imagine an anchoress enjoying explaining to others what to do or how they have erred or being mysterious and above reproach. Julian's writings tell us that she was not like this at all; she overflowed with a passionate belief in God's love for all.

Human beings seem to have an inborn desire to see others punished and often believe the same thing about God. In Julian's time, the fourteenth and early fifteenth centuries, the Church was particularly bent on images of a vengeful God set on judgment and punishment. Julian, however, after a near-death illness, had visions of a dif-ferent God, a God who was loving, "courteous," and full of grace. She called Jesus "Mother" and saw Christ's love graphically poured out for others through his blood and suffering. She saw God tenderly holding the world in the divine hand like a hazelnut. Julian wrote, "And when we be thus strengthened by His sweet working, then we with all our will choose Him, by His sweet grace, to be His servants and His lovers lastingly without end."[5]

Even though the door to her cell was bolted shut, Julian's hospitality is why we still know who she is; the manuscripts of her visions were kept by others and, over time, copied and preserved. Margery Kempe, another medieval woman writer, was impressed enough by her visit to Julian that she included it in her autobiography.[6] For Julian, a life of solitude was a gift she held in trust and gave away to her neighbors.

Questions for Reflection

1. Toward what sorts of people do you tend to feel the most judgmental and resentful? How could you use time in solitude to get more deeply in touch with God's love for those people?
2. What does it mean to you that your solitude is something you do not for yourself alone, but something you hold in trust for your neighbor? For the world?

 # WEDNESDAY: MOSES AND THE VEIL

Whenever Moses went into the LORD's presence to speak with him, Moses would take the veil off until he came out again. When Moses came out and told the Israelites what he had been commanded, the Israelites would see that the skin of Moses' face was shining brightly. So Moses would put the veil on his face again until the next time he went in to speak with the LORD.

—Exodus 34:34–35 (CEB)

Moses had been in the wilderness with his people for over a year by the time he ascended Mount Sinai to receive the law from God. He and the Israelites had seen danger, hardship, and many wonders as they crossed the desert to Sinai. Many more years lay ahead—thirty-nine, in fact—before they would reach God's promised land. Moses would die before their journey ended; meanwhile, he was their long-suffering pastor, expedition leader, and overwhelmed ombudsman.

Moses was probably an introvert. He carefully, quietly killed an Egyptian man he witnessed beating a Hebrew slave. When he realized his crime had been discovered, he escaped, alone, into the desert. There, he married and became a shepherd, a lonely job with lots of time for introspection. One day while out with the family sheep, he all but tripped over a burning bush and heard God's voice ordering him to step out of his sandals. God then called him to a very noncontemplative task—to confront the pharaoh and lead his people out of slavery. Notably, here the bulk of Moses' conversation with God involved anxiously asking just how he would do this, what would he say, and how would he say it?

Without a charismatic, confrontational personality, there was not much to keep the Israelites from complaining about Moses' lack of leadership or from blaming him for everything that went wrong once they were all out in the desert. This must have been an utterly exhausting time for Moses, used to being alone with his sheep. When he and the Israelites finally reached Sinai and God invited him to some time alone in the divine presence on top of the mountain, it probably sounded like a welcome respite.

However, the time Moses spent with God was not actually for reverie or refreshment; it was hard work. Moses' solitude with God was not for himself but for his people, as he received and recorded the law that God was giving them. This was not new; earlier in their journey, the Israelites had expressly asked Moses to shield them from the intensity of the presence of God, to act as their mediator (Exod. 20:19). As if the rest of his service and generosity were not enough, later, when Moses' face shone brightly (or grew horns, as older translations famously interpreted) as a result of his time with God, he courteously wore a veil around the camp when he was not teaching the law, a small but sacrificial gesture of modesty and hospitality since the Israelites were disturbed and unsettled by his glow.

Hospitality can be a quality of our relationships and leadership, not just of the physical space of our homes and churches. Moses set part of himself aside—even the glow of his personal relationship with God—so that other people would feel welcome and comfortable in his physical presence. He was an approachable leader, even when he had every right to be formidable. Perhaps he drew deeply on the well of his solitude with God, both from his time as a shepherd and his time on Mount Sinai. The solitude he was privileged to share with God was the source of both his leadership and hospitality, even in something as small as covering his face with a veil to put his people at ease in his presence.

Questions for Reflection

1. What is a time that you may have "veiled" yourself in order to put others at ease? How is veiling yourself out of shame different from veiling yourself out of hospitality or service? What are some examples?

2. Rather than an escape or a rest, have you ever thought about time in prayerful solitude as something that may in fact become a gift for others? How could your time spent in solitude with God be a gift for your coworkers, your family, your congregation, or your friends?

THURSDAY: ANNA
THE PROPHET

[Anna] never left the temple but worshiped there with fasting and prayer night and day. At that moment she came, and began to praise God and to speak about the child [Jesus] to all who were looking for the redemption of Jerusalem.

—Luke 2:37b–38

Be like those who are waiting for their master to return from the wedding banquet, so that they may open the door for him as soon as he comes and knocks.

—Luke 12:36

The gospel of Luke only briefly mentions the life of Anna, an elderly woman who welcomed Jesus, Mary, and Joseph to the temple at Jerusalem when they came to make an offering after Jesus' birth. Still, Luke includes many particular details about her: the name of her father, her tribe, and her age (eighty-four or over one hundred, depending on your reading). He explains that she was a widow who lived in the temple and "worshiped there with fasting and prayer, night and day." All Luke tells us about Simeon, the Jewish elder also on the scene that day, is that he was righteous and happened to stop by the temple at the same time as the Holy Family.

What made Anna so interesting and special? How did she manage to live at the temple? Did she have a consecrated space of some kind, like Julian's anchorage? Could she have been part of a community or order of widows? Had she shown up for prayer one day, years before, and never left? Regardless, rather than keeping solitude in her home, in a cave in the desert, or even a monastic community like the Essenes, Anna chose to live a consecrated religious life inside the temple itself, where she would be close to the Holy of Holies but also to the priests and worshipers there. Her solitude there was part of something larger and could easily be a gift to others.

She would have been in the habit of welcoming and greeting visitors, as well as praying and fasting. Jesus may not have been the first baby she greeted, but Luke is clear that it was her spiritual discipline that allowed her to recognize this baby as the Messiah, in a way that even Mary and Joseph didn't.[7]

Anna's solitude and hospitality, practiced for decades in the midst of the busy Jerusalem temple, gave her a special attentiveness to the people she met. This in turn prepared her to be one of the first people to witness to the miracle of the incarnation. Simone Weil wrote, "Attention is the rarest and purest form of generosity."[8] Solitude can nurture in us the ability to deeply feel God's presence and so too to generously and deeply see other people. In the temple, Anna gave the attention of her mind and body to not only God but also the people who came there, both great and humble — eventually including Christ himself.

Questions for Reflection

1. Simone Weil also wrote, "Absolutely unmixed attention is prayer."[9] What do these and her above words about attention and generosity say to you in your own life? How do they relate or not relate to your own prayer life right now?
2. Do you feel you have "seen" God or Christ in your life of prayer or hospitality to other people? If so, how would you describe it? If not, do you expect to?

 FRIDAY FASTING: HUNGER

Skip Lunch

He who fasts and does not do good, saves his bread but loses his soul.
> —A Handbook of Proverbs (1855)[10]

Look, you serve your own interest on your fast day,
and oppress all your workers.
> —Isaiah 58:3b

Inspiration

Fasting for inner, spiritual growth without turning outward where so many of God's people live in hunger is self-defeating. Scripture scolds religious people for fasting for personal gain or for the sake of a righteous appearance while neglecting to live a life according to the justice and mercy that God has commanded. Religious teachers have cautioned against the temptation to use fasting as a way to save money or as a way to lose weight. Augustine of Hippo preached, "Your distress will [only] profit you if you afford comfort to others."[11]

Fasting is about prayer, but it's also about feeling *hungry.* Irish Catholic historian Eamon Duffy lamented the loss of regular fasting in the Roman Catholic Church, not for the sake of personal penance but for the "prophetic witness of the whole community—the matter-of-fact witness, repeated week by week, that to be Christian is to stand among the needy."[12] Solitude also means solidarity and the vulnerability of standing close to the needy. How can your fasting be a witness and connection to the hungry?

Practice

Skip lunch. Go somewhere you can spend some time and energy in reading and prayer about local and global hunger issues. You could go online to learn about situations and charities in your local community or to your favorite news source to learn about people in the world suffering from famine or food shortages right now. Pray in solidarity with your hungry neighbors and the charities that serve them.

If at all possible, do not announce or reveal your fast to others outside your immediate family, if even them. If skipping lunch would be too noticeable, skip dinner or breakfast instead. Through your hunger, open yourself to compassion and prayer for people who are hungry every day. *If there is any reason fasting from food may not be good for your health, do not fast but simply pray as described.*

Questions for Reflection

1. How did fasting in solidarity with the hungry feel different from fasting on previous Fridays? Was it easier or harder for you with this emphasis? Did you feel moved to give to any charities you encountered? (If so, make that part of your almsgiving this week.)
2. Did it help you deepen in solitude with God, or was it just inconvenient?

SATURDAY ALMSGIVING: FOOD FOR THE HUNGRY

*If you offer your food to the hungry
and satisfy the needs of the afflicted,*

then your light shall rise in the darkness
and your gloom be like the noonday.
　　　　　　　　—Isaiah 58:10

For I was hungry and you gave me food, I was thirsty and
you gave me something to drink, I was a stranger and you
welcomed me.
　　　　　　　　—Matthew 25:35

Choose the form of almsgiving you will practice this week
or, if it gives you joy, do both. Give an amount that feels
generous and "hurts" a little in the context of your weekly
expenses. Grow in solitude by giving to others.

1. Give cash away to someone who asks you for it.
2. Mail a check or give online to a hunger organization.
   As you have been pondering and praying about hospitality this week, offer the most basic gift of hospitality
   we can make to anyone, and direct your almsgiving
   toward food for the hungry. Make a special Lenten
   gift to help those who fast because they don't have any
   choice or who rarely or never have the ability to host
   a meal for someone else because they don't even have
   enough for themselves:
   — a local food pantry or soup kitchen
   — a global food aid organization

Questions for Reflection

1. Does generosity make you feel rich or poor this week?
   Does it feel like a spiritual act?
2. How did you choose where to give your alms this
   week?
3. Did giving make more space within you for the presence of God? How?

WEEK FIVE

SOLITUDE AND RESISTANCE

SUNDAY: JESUS WITHDREW

But he would withdraw to deserted places and pray.
—Luke 5:16

Acquire a peaceful spirit, and around you thousands will be saved.

—Seraphim of Sarov[1]

Perhaps peace is not, after all, something you work for, or "fight for." It is indeed "fighting for peace" that starts all the wars. . . . If you are yourself at peace, then there is at least some peace in the world. . . . But I am not speaking of quietism, because quietism is not peace, nor is it the way to peace.
—Thomas Merton, *Conjectures of a Guilty Bystander*

Can solitude be a political act? Choosing to live as a solitary or hermit can seem like a turning away from society, but many religious people who have lived in solitude and contemplation have also been great resisters of the powers and principalities of their day. From a quiet life herding sheep in the desert, Moses had a vision that drove him to face down pharaoh. John Chrysostom spent two years as a hermit before becoming a bishop who preached against the corruption of wealth and enacted dramatic church reforms. Cuthbert of Lindisfarne was a monk who became a bishop; then he became a hermit again, then a bishop again, and then back to being a hermit, until his death. Seraphim of Sarov broke his solitude to return to his monastery to be available to guests, often soldiers. Howard Thurman, a mystic and theologian, was an early advocate of nonviolence and a mentor to The Rev. Dr. Martin Luther King Jr. Thomas Merton lived as a hermit on the property of his monastery but also wrote popular books and essays against white supremacy and the Vietnam War.

Jesus withdrew into solitude from both the crowds and his ministry, regularly, to pray and rest. He addressed the powers and principalities at the temple and the palace, but he also withdrew from those circles of power in favor of small towns, rural roads, and forgotten corners of Jerusalem. He healed and spoke to many whom his friends and family would have considered "the enemy." He chose to not speak at all sometimes. He practiced resistance by withdrawing—from crowds, from circles of power, and from acts of violence. To resist means both to create an opposing force and to withstand force exerted on you. It can be active and passive, apostolic and contemplative.

Choosing to spend time in solitude and prayer is something that most of the world considers unproductive, lonely, even pathetic. Prayer and solitude may seem the inverse of resistance, confrontation, and protest, but, in fact, they are powerful instruments for social change and nonviolent activism. The Rev. Dr. Martin Luther King Jr. puts it this way: "Peace is not merely a distant goal that we seek, but a means by which we arrive at that goal."[2] Prayer and solitude grounds our mind, heart, and soul in the peace and love of Christ. Prayer and solitude also are how we invite the Holy Spirit to direct us through the wisdom of intuition and divine guidance. The power of prayer and the movement of the Holy Spirit can truly change systems of power and injustice that seem otherwise entrenched. However, prayer and solitude must not lead us to quietism or isolationism, as Merton warns above, but through Christ to resistance and truth.

When Jesus stood to be interrogated before Pilate, he resisted, but he didn't fight back. He didn't choose to best his opponent with wordplay, signs and wonders, or lawyers. He stood as a quiet, nonviolent witness against everything that Pilate and the religious establishment stood for: the will to power, conformity, self-preservation. Jesus didn't win his case, but his conviction and crucifixion were the entrance of the living God into the pain and suffering of humanity. Resistance and love led Jesus to crucifixion but also finally to resurrection, and eventually turned a whole empire upside down. His death and resurrection were God's response of love and forgiveness: a divine but subversive resistance to human evil and violence.

Questions for Reflection

1. What comes more naturally to you: *doing* or *being*? How could a practice of solitude give your *doing* more peace, in the spirit of the above quotation by Seraphim of Sarov, or your *being* more resistance, in the spirit of the quotation by Thomas Merton?

2. When can silence be used most effectively as resistance? What are some examples? When should silence not be used as resistance?

Choose a Practice for This Week

— Use silence and solitude this week in response to offense, overwhelming pain, or posturing. If someone criticizes or insults you, respond with silence. If you notice you are angry, give yourself a "timeout" and walk away. This is not to give anyone "the silent treatment" but to step back from debate, defensiveness, overengagement, and overfunctioning. What do you notice? How is it challenging? How is it satisfying?

— Spend ten to twenty minutes in quiet solitude, either in meditation, prayer, coloring, or looking out a window. Then sit down and handwrite a letter to one of your elected officials, addressing an issue in the news that has been of particular concern to you. Express your concern, anger, or fear from a place of love and compassion but also with firmness and the fullness of your conviction. If you feel so moved, refer to your faith and the season of Lent. End by thanking the official for his or her work and public service. Send the letter and pray for that official for a day or a week.

 # MONDAY: JOHN THE BAPTIST

The child grew and became strong in spirit, and he was in the wilderness until the day he appeared publicly to Israel.
—Luke 1:80

As they went away, Jesus began to speak to the crowds about John: "What did you go out into the wilderness to look at? A reed shaken by the wind?"

—Matthew 11:7

For Herod feared John, knowing that he was a righteous and holy man, and he protected him. When he heard him, he was greatly perplexed; and yet he liked to listen to him.

—Mark 6:20

John the Baptist lived alone in the desert for many years before he reappeared near the Jordan River, preaching up a storm to any and all who would listen. Luke hints in 1:80 (see above) that he was just a kid (a teenager? even younger?) when he took off for the wilds of Judea. What drove him off?

As the son of a priest, John was probably often at the temple. As he grew up in its orbit, he would have become aware of the mysterious nature of the presence of God. He would also have seen the longing and hunger of the people who came for worship and the ugly underbelly of religious politics. It's hard to imagine that he wouldn't have had a rebellious, truth-telling spirit even as a child—and a "pastor's kid," at that. It seems likely that all these things would have conspired to drive him out into the wilderness. There, he could pursue the presence of God undistracted, with the persecuted people of Jerusalem in his mind's eye, free of the oversight of the temple hierarchy and from folks who might say, "Aren't you Zechariah's son?" It could be that Zechariah and Elizabeth were just as happy to see him take off for the desert, for his sake and theirs.

John fits our classic stereotype of the eccentric hermit: he wore animal skins, ate bugs, and had a cantankerous personality. When he left the desert and appeared at the Jordan, however, he emerged as a prophet par excellence. He skirted the edges of society, called men and women to repent, and said harsh, unpleasant things to the beautiful and powerful. He was a gadfly at the heel of King Herod Antipas, though as Mark coyly comments: "When [Herod] heard him, he was greatly perplexed; and yet he liked to listen to him" (6:20). Despite his crazy-prophet look and rabble-rousing, there must have been something compelling about John the Baptist, if even Herod, the greatest target of his fury, found his preaching compelling and acted to protect him, at least for a while.

John the Baptist wasn't only a revolutionary activist; he was a deeply spiritual and religious man who spent years of his life in solitude. He sounds arrogant and self-righteous in his calls to repentance, but he was actually full of humility: "I am not worthy to stoop down and untie the thong of [Jesus'] sandals," (Mark 1:7) and "He must increase, but I must decrease" (John 3:30). He was grounded in who he was and he knew who he was not.

Spending time in contemplative solitude does not mean growing in serenity at the expense of truth-telling. It is medicine for pride and ego, and it feeds integrity. John the Baptist was a prophet whose voice was grounded in the years he spent alone in the wilderness with God, willing to sacrifice his solitude, his safety, and, finally, his life, to speak truth to power.

Questions for Reflection

1. Have you known leaders who were both great contemplatives and great activists? What did you most admire about them?
2. What truth-telling might God be calling you to in your life right now? How might growing in solitude help you grow in courage to do so? In humility?

TUESDAY: CATHERINE OF SIENA

I am now rejoicing in my sufferings for your sake, and in my flesh I am completing what is lacking in Christ's afflictions for the sake of his body, that is, the church.

—Colossians 1:24

We've had enough exhortations to be silent. Cry out with a thousand tongues—I see the world is rotten because of silence.

—Catherine of Siena

Catherine of Siena spent three years living as a solitary in a three-by-nine-foot closet in her family's home. Since childhood, she felt an intimate sense of the presence of God. Her parents tried for years to respectably marry her off, but she was able to convince them she wanted to be a contemplative nun and nothing else. She was veiled as a third-order Dominican when she was sixteen and devoted herself to prayer, fasting, and visions, leaving her closet only to attend Mass.

Despite her vocation as a contemplative, Catherine wasn't a quiet or peaceful person; she was fierce and passionate. She practiced harsh, physical acts of penance, which were common at that time: extreme fasting, whipping herself, wearing an iron chain as a girdle, and keeping long vigils, or praying instead of sleeping. It's hard to grasp a person like Catherine, whose heartfelt spiritual disciplines are unfathomable to modern sensibilities. However, the intensity of these spiritual and physical workouts built her endurance, self-confidence, and what seems to have been a bottomless capability to love others, which finally swelled to overflowing in that tiny cell.

After three years in her inner room, where Jesus met her every day in prayer and visions, the day came where Catherine realized he was standing outside the door. He invited her to come out, to grow in her love for him even more by loving others. So, slowly, she began to move into public life: first by simply walking downstairs to join her family for dinner, then helping her mother around the house, and before long, walking the streets to serve the poor and sick of Siena. Her circle of love and service continued to widen, as did her renown, until she was being asked to mediate between spouses, parents and children, and even whole feuding families. The bandwidth of her care and concern increased to include the most significant feuding family in medieval Europe—the Church.

The fourteenth century was a time of unprecedented turmoil for Western Christendom. In 1307, for political reasons, the pope left Rome and moved to Avignon, in present-day France. Clergy across Europe were being ordained without education or training and clerical corruption was rampant. Italy, home of the Vatican, boiled with violence and war. Catherine became involved in all these issues, exchanging hundreds of letters with people of influence, both men and women: the pope, kings, cardinals, military commanders, and Italian aristocrats. She petitioned Pope Gregory XI again and again to move back to Rome. He finally did, due in no small way to Catherine's never-ending stream of letters and rebukes.

Catherine spent three years in silence with God in a closet of her family's home, but she didn't stay there. She poured herself out as a libation, bestowing comfort, counsel, and prophetic rebuke to persons great and humble. She died young—at thirty-three—almost certainly because of her lifelong practice of extreme fasting and vigils, as well as the stress and strain of her constant service and self-giving to so many people and political concerns. Perhaps she lived as long as she did in spite of all those things because of her relationship with Jesus Christ, a deep well of love and integrity formed in the years she spent in solitude with him.

Questions for Reflection

1. One of Catherine's most famous quotations is, "Be who God meant you to be and you will set the world on fire." What is it that "God meant you to be," that perhaps you are suppressing or ignoring right now in your life? How could *being* "who God meant you to be" serve as a form of resistance to the status quo or oppression of others you see in your context? In your workplace? In your church community?

2. Have you noticed that increased solitude in your life has led to increased love and ability to "resist"? How? If not, do some thinking about what else is at play spiritually in your life right now that may be hindering you from becoming "who God meant you to be."

WEDNESDAY: HOWARD THURMAN

In the morning, while it was still very dark, he got up and went out to a deserted place, and there he prayed.
—Mark 1:35

Of all weapons, love is the most deadly and devastating, and few there be who dare trust their fate in its hands.
—Howard Thurman, *Deep Is the Hunger*

Howard Thurman didn't live as a solitary or a hermit. He was a married man with children and a career as an academic and a pastor; but he lived a deeply contemplative life and became renowned as a teacher and theologian, especially among leaders of the civil rights movement. Most notably, The Rev. Dr. Martin Luther King Jr. King was said to have carried a copy of Thurman's *Jesus and the Disinherited* along with him throughout the Montgomery bus boycott.

Thurman's great concern, as he wrote in that book, was for "what the teachings and life of Jesus have to say to those who stand, at a moment in human history, with their backs against the wall."[3] He wondered how an oppressed people, in particular black Americans, could survive spiritually without being irrevocably damaged by fear, denial, and hatred (he devoted a chapter to each in that book), natural reactions to living surrounded by the pernicious racism of our nation. As an adult, Thurman gave a copy of his book *Deep River* to young Martin and Coretta King as a gift and wrote on the flyleaf, "The test of life is often found in the amount of pain we can absorb without spoiling our joy."[4]

Thurman was born in 1899 and grew up in segregated Daytona Beach, Florida, at that time a small town. Even as a child, he was a mystic, always feeling the presence of God close by. He would talk to the ocean and with an old oak tree, which he liked to watch in storm season, "moving and absorbing all the violence of the wind." He spoke of "the dark nights and the quiet roar of the Atlantic . . . I had a sense of being a part of this whole rhythmic flow of life. My earliest religious experience was identified with that sort of thing. So that I would talk aloud to God . . . in that setting. . . . This had more religious meaning for me than the things that happened in church."[5] Still, he recalls in his autobiography how his local congregation shaped him, "the watchful attention of my sponsors in the church served to enhance my consciousness that whatever I did with my life *mattered*."[6]

Prayer and mysticism were as central to Thurman's writing, teaching, and speaking as nonviolence. He wrote continually about the value of contemplation to self, others, and the wider community. He gave advice to King along these lines, traveling to visit him after King was stabbed at a book signing. He urged King to minister to his interior self, that this was crucial to the health of the wider movement: [I urged him to take] "time away from the immediate pressure of the movement to reassess himself in relation to the cause, to rest his body and mind with healing detachment, and to take a long look that only solitary brooding can provide."[7] King followed Thurman's advice, taking twice as long away from public life as his doctor had recommended.

Solitude, according to Thurman, is the place we find God and our truest selves. Solitude is where we can find the inner resources to face hatred and oppression and to survive intact as children of God.

Questions for Reflection

1. In times of trial or testing, do you take time out for "solitary brooding"? How? If not, how might you take Thurman's advice when future challenges arise? What does "solitary brooding" mean to you, exactly, and how would you define its purpose? Can it also hinder?
2. Thurman believed that the most effective resistance takes place when we are secure in our self-identity and our ability to absorb pain. Do you agree? Why or why not?

THURSDAY: CHARLES DE FOUCAULD

Those who say, "I love God," and hate their brothers or sisters, are liars; for those who do not love a brother or sister whom they have seen, cannot love God whom they have not seen.

—1 John 4:20

I no longer want a monastery that is too secure; I want a small monastery, like the house of a poor workman who is not sure if tomorrow he will find work and bread, who with all his being shares the suffering of the world.

—Charles de Foucauld

When Charles de Foucauld was in military school as a young man, his nickname was "Piggy." He was a big spender, a lover of food and wine, and so plump that his school uniforms had to be special-ordered. He was a terrible student, a lazy soldier, and not religious whatsoever. On a series of postings in North Africa in the 1880s, he was intrigued by the faith of the Jews and Muslims there. Then, during a trip home to France, he had a conversion experience. His passion for comforts became a passion for the imitation of Christ. First, he tried his vocation with Trappist monks, but he wanted more rigor (it gives you a sense of his intensity that the Trappists weren't rigorous enough for him). More important, he didn't want to be stuck inside a cloister but to know his neighbors and to serve them.

Charles found his way back to his beloved North Africa. He wanted to live as Jesus did at Nazareth, in poverty, manual labor, and prayer, and he began to call himself "Charles of Jesus." He was a man with competing desires; he longed to be completely alone with God but also to welcome and serve all. He wanted to live in complete poverty; but his considerable fortune funded his life and generosity, allowing him to buy food and medicine, land and building supplies for his hermitages and otherwise to care for his neighbors, including some whom he bought and liberated from slavery.

Edward Saïd once said that every turn-of-the-century European was, at bottom, "a racist, an imperialist, and almost totally ethnocentric."[8] Similarly, Charles's mission, as he described it in many cringe-worthy letters, was to invite "barbaric" Muslims into the civility of French culture and to true belief in Jesus Christ. However, unlike the government, military, or other missionaries of his time, Charles sought to colonize through friendship and servanthood. He was a living example of both solitude and solidarity. He spent a lot of time alone and a lot of time with his neighbors. He lived in the same huts as they did. He spoke Arabic and Tuareg. He cooked and did laundry for the poor with his own hands. He ate the simplest of foods, wore sandals and ratty robes, and became gaunt and scraggly; no longer the dapper, chubby "Piggy" of his youth. He was loved by his neighbors, and he truly loved them. One Muslim neighbor told a friend of Charles's: "How terrible it is to think that such a good man will go to hell when he dies because he is not a Muslim."[9]

Charles lived the last five years of his life in three places: a hermitage outside the village of Tamanrasset, Algeria, a second hermitage that was a four-day journey into the Ahaggar Mountains, and inside a fort. During the First World War, instead of packing up for home or a military base, he used his wealth to build the fort where he and his neighbors in Tamanrasset could take shelter. Tragically, in 1916, he died right outside of its walls, shot in panic by a fifteen-year-old bandit.

Although Charles mostly lived as a hermit, his life was political by its very nature. In some ways, he was an instrument of the French Empire. In other ways, he was a subversive—a one-man movement, a mole for Christ—beholding the Muslims he encountered not as potential converts but as people and seeing his future bound up with theirs, come what may.

Questions for Reflection

1. People are generally either entranced or repulsed by Charles de Foucauld; how do you feel about him? What do you most admire about his practice of solitude and resistance, and what do you question?
2. How could Foucauld be helpful as a patron saint for Christian-Muslim relations? How could he be a roadblock?

FRIDAY FASTING: POVERTY

Fast from Purchasing

. . . as poor, yet making many rich; as having nothing, and yet possessing everything.

—2 Corinthians 6:10b

Poverty is the way to salvation, the nurse of humility, and the root of perfection. Its fruits are hidden, but they multiply themselves infinite ways.

—Francis of Assisi, in a letter

Inspiration

One of the most immediate ways you can choose to stand in solitude from the powers and principalities at work in society is to attempt to get through a day without using money. Participating in commerce isn't a sin, but money is power: to provide for ourselves, to solve problems, to access health care, to seek justice. To go through a single day noticing how often you pay for the needs and wants of daily life reveals your everyday connections to that power, as well as the time savings and other benefits that come with it. It's also a reminder that there are other ways (often better ways than spending money) to solve the most pressing problems of our lives.

Poverty is not enjoyable; neither is fasting, but just as fasting can remind us that we are always hungry, choosing poverty as a spiritual discipline can remind us that we are always poor, except in Christ.

Practice

Do not purchase, shop, or participate in money changing hands today, if at all possible. Whenever you have an option, choose the solitude and solidarity of poverty. Consider whether you should pack your lunch, fill your car with gas, or make other preparations in advance. Do not ask other people to buy things for you, but do not refuse a gift; if the fast will cause you to be inhospitable in any way, break it. If at all possible, do not announce or reveal your fast to others outside your immediate family, if even them.

Questions for Reflection

1. Was it possible to get through a day without participating in a purchase? What did you notice about using money on a daily basis that you might not have realized before?
2. Did it help you deepen in solitude with God, or was it just inconvenient?

SATURDAY ALMSGIVING: JUSTICE

Is not this the fast that I choose:
to loose the bonds of injustice,
to undo the thongs of the yoke,
to let the oppressed go free,
and to break every yoke?
— Isaiah 58:6

He has told you, O mortal, what is good;
and what does the LORD require of you
but to do justice, and to love kindness,
and to walk humbly with your God?

— Micah 6:8

Choose the form of almsgiving you will practice this week or, if it gives you joy, do both. Give an amount that feels generous and "hurts" a little in the context of your weekly expenses. Grow in solitude by giving to others.

1. Give cash away to someone who asks you for it.
2. Mail a check or give online to a civil rights organization. Solitude is not about building a wall to shield or to insulate us from the hurts and suffering of the world but to strengthen us to seek more effectively for the kingdom of God and to work for the good of others. Charles de Foucauld, Howard Thurman, Catherine of Siena, and John the Baptist all stood on a foundation of solitude to speak up about injustice to the leaders of their time. They stood up for the needy and the forgotten and called the wealthy and powerful to be accountable. How can you do the same, this Lent and beyond? Consider making a Lenten gift to an organization that

does the same for a group or cause that is particularly meaningful to you:
— a local organization that advocates for a minority group in your community
— an organization that offers legal aid and assistance to those who might otherwise be unable to afford or access it
— a national civil rights organization

Questions for Reflection

1. Does generosity make you feel rich or poor this week? Does it feel like a spiritual act?
2. How did you choose where to give your alms this week?
3. Did giving make more space within you for the presence of God?

HOLY WEEK

SOLITUDE AND CONFINEMENT

PALM SUNDAY: IMPRISONMENT

*So they took Jeremiah and threw him into the cistern . . .
letting Jeremiah down by ropes. Now there was no water in
the cistern, but only mud, and Jeremiah sank in the mud.*

—Jeremiah 38:6

*They seized him and led him away, bringing him into the
high priest's house.*

—Luke 22:54a

I am counted among those who go down to the Pit;
I am like those who have no help,
like those forsaken among the dead,
like the slain that lie in the grave.

—Psalm 88:4–5

Imprisonment is forced solitude. There is a long history in the Christian tradition of deeply faithful people who have gone to prison. While there, some have performed miracles—for instance, Daniel in the lions' den and Peter jailed in Jerusalem. Others have written religious texts that have been treasured by generations of other believers—Paul imprisoned in Rome, Martin Luther in Wartburg Castle, and Martin Luther King Jr. in his *Letter from a Birmingham Jail*. Some even transformed their nations or church history from behind prison bars—like Joseph in pharaoh's prison in Egypt, Dietrich Bonhoeffer in a Nazi prison in Berlin, and Nelson Mandela on Robben Island and at Victor Verster in South Africa.

Jesus was imprisoned the night he was arrested. The details are barely suggested in the Gospels but can be glimpsed a small gap in the action, before or after his trial by the temple priests, depending on the Gospel. There's a tradition in Jerusalem dating back to the fourth century that associates the ruins of an underground dungeon with the house of Caiaphas, the chief priest. Ever since, pilgrims have climbed down its stone steps to see rock caverns where prisoners were chained, to pray and commemorate the night Jesus may have spent there. There is a deep pit there, like the cistern where Jeremiah is described as having been imprisoned. This pit has only a narrow opening at its top and opens downward into the rock. In the church built above, there's a mosaic showing Jesus in that pit with a rope harness around his shoulders to help visitors imagine that, like Jeremiah, he could have been lowered down into the cell like a bucket into a well.

Imprisonment can manifest as a prison cell, enslavement, a physical or mental illness, or any confining circumstances beyond our control. In the practice of solitude, as in the practice of fasting, our humility and compassion can grow when we pray from awareness of those whose lives are the inverse of ours or the inverse of a particular spiritual discipline. When you fast, remember the hungry. In solitude, especially during Holy Week, hold in prayer those who are confined to a solitude they didn't choose, whose time alone has been forced on them and perhaps involves violence, humiliation, or even torture.

There are moments in human life without hope. Peter and Paul experienced the miraculous grace of being freed by angels, but more often, prison is a misery, the darkness of the Pit or the brutal "refiner's fire" of the psalmist.[1] Sometimes, it can transform people—like Martin Luther or Malcolm X—but sometimes, it can destroy them, like Thomas More or John the Baptist.

No one would choose a transformation through imprisonment, but a life without freedom or safety is a reality for many people, whether in a prison cell, through human trafficking, or some other form of entrapment. We are never trapped in a solitude that is beyond God's reach, however. God is sovereign, even in the face of terrible captivity, and goes with human beings into every prison, physical or spiritual, whether or not there is hope of freedom one day. Jesus went through imprisonment only to be sent to his crucifixion; but on the other side, after anguish and death, God's power brought him to resurrection. May you feel both righteous anger and compassion for those trapped in prison. May you feel hope for them and for yourself, whatever entrapment you may face in your own life.

Questions for Reflection

1. Have you ever been jailed? Do you know anyone who is or has been in jail? Do you have other familiarity with what physical captivity is like? How is physical captivity similar to spiritual captivity, and how is it different?

2. What spiritual imprisonments are you aware of in your life right now? Do you have hope for freedom from this imprisonment one day? What are you doing to survive your spiritual captivity, spiritually or otherwise?

Choose a Practice for This Week

— Meditate on Psalm 88 (quoted above). Set aside twenty to thirty minutes of solitude in a quiet place and do some *lectio divina*, or holy reading. Use some or all of these prompts:
  - Invite the Holy Spirit to join you.
  - Copy the verses in your own handwriting, no matter how bad it is, either in your journal or on any piece of paper.
  - Read them aloud.
  - Draw or doodle around them.
  - Reflect or journal:
    ❖ What phrases particularly draw your attention?
    ❖ What are you feeling about imprisonment and loneliness in your own life right now?
    ❖ What might God be trying to say to you through these words in response?
    ❖ What aspect of the imprisonment of others might God be calling you to pray for or be present to?
    ❖ What might God be inviting you to pray for or be present to this Holy Week?
    ❖ What does the resurrection mean to you this week?
  - As you bring this time to a close, either read aloud or write out the verses once more.
  - Finally, pray for prisoners and captives, especially those in solitary confinement.
— Go to the website of the nearest jail or prison. Learn about the kinds of prisoners housed there, the services provided, when and how families can visit inmates, what volunteers are sought, and other details the website might provide. Use this information as a basis for prayer. You might use the prayer "For Prisons and Correctional Institutions" from *The Book of Common Prayer*:

Lord Jesus, for our sake you were condemned as a criminal: Visit our jails and prisons with your pity and judgment. Remember all prisoners, and bring the guilty to repentance and amendment of life according to your will, and give them hope for their future. When any are held unjustly, bring them release; forgive us, and teach us to improve our justice. Remember those who work in these institutions; keep them humane and compassionate; and save them from becoming brutal or callous. And since what we do for those in prison, O Lord, we do for you, constrain us to improve their lot. All this we ask for your mercy's sake. *Amen.* (p. 826)

MONDAY: DANIEL IN THE LIONS' DEN

Then the king gave the command, and Daniel was brought and thrown into the den of lions. The king said to Daniel, "May your God, whom you faithfully serve, deliver you!"
—Daniel 6:16

Didn't my Lord deliver Daniel? And why not every man?
—African American Spiritual

The story of Daniel in the lions' den is one of the classics of Bible storybooks for kids. There's a brave man, a bad king, some fierce beasts, and a cave littered with bones and puddles of blood. The story was probably first written down[2] by the Jewish people living under the Seleucid Empire in the second century BCE, but like many folk stories, it's set in a heroic past, distant from the too-real violence of its present day. The Jews, like Daniel in the lions' den, felt trapped, unjustly persecuted, and very much alone. So, they told a story to help them survive.

Daniel's imprisonment and miraculous survival is the stuff of tall tales but has held deep meaning for oppressed and suffering people in both Jewish and Christian history. The Jews suffered terribly under Seleucid rule: men, women, and children were massacred; the emperor had a pig slaughtered in the Holy of Holies; he made circumcision, Sabbath-keeping, and the possession of Torah scrolls and holy books punishable by death. Centuries later, enslaved Black Americans heard God speaking to them, too, in the story of Daniel, composing spirituals that declared: "Didn't my Lord deliver Daniel?" and "God had sent His angel down to lock the lions' jaws." The story of Daniel is not just for children, or even for struggling individuals, but one that whole communities of people have leaned on for spiritual survival in the face of oppression and violence.

Daniel was living as a Jew in Persia. When King Darius made foreign prayers illegal, Daniel went to his room to pray, facing Jerusalem, as he always had, and faced the consequences. The story of Daniel is about being who God made us to be and knowing that we can be punished for being faithful—punished, in a way, for being our truest selves. King Darius sent Daniel to the lions' den, but the hungry forces of death symbolized by the lions did not lay tooth or claw on him. In one rabbinic midrash, they lick and cuddle with him like kittens. When Darius returned and rolled the stone away (note the connection Christians would later make to the empty tomb), there was Daniel, safe and sound. Then, in the way of classic morality tales, the conniving scribes and their families were thrown into the pit instead, where all were gobbled up.

We all wish a night spent in a dark prison might end this way, even if only in our daydreams; that we would emerge completely unscathed and victorious, our enemies thrown to fierce beasts. In reality, dark nights and lions' dens rarely have just, simple, or happy endings. And yet, when we're facing down the forces of death and destruction in our lives or communities and feeling trapped in a solitude we did not choose, we, like Daniel, can hope to hold onto our identity and our faith in the midst of great threat, to survive with trust in God's ultimate power and with our integrity intact.

Questions for Reflection

1. Have you ever felt trapped and alone in a "lions' den"? What put you in that kind of position? What delivered you? Did you feel as though God was absent? Or with you?
2. Are you or have you even been part of a community that could have used a good sermon on the story of Daniel to hold on to faith, integrity, or hope in the midst of danger or some kind of imprisonment? How might the story speak to your community particularly?

TUESDAY: JOHN OF PATMOS

I, John, your brother who share with you in Jesus the persecution and the kingdom and the patient endurance, was on the island called Patmos because of the word of God and the testimony of Jesus.

—Revelation 1:9

Banishment is imprisonment in reverse. Instead of confining a prisoner in a cell, a prisoner must "get out and stay out." John of Patmos was exiled to the remote island of Patmos, part of a group of islands the ancient Romans called the *Sporades* or "those scattered" outside the more trafficked island groups of the Aegean. The Romans made a habit of banishing anyone who threatened the order and authority of the empire, often sending troublemakers to its obscure corners rather than beyond its borders, perhaps better to keep an eye on them.

John's prison was a beautiful island with rolling hills, rocky outcroppings, and views of the sea. All things considered, he had it pretty good. Still, he was trapped and far from family, friends, and the places he knew. We don't know if he was alone there or in the company of other exiled Christians (there is an Orthodox tradition that the deacon Prochorus[3] worked as his secretary). Whether or not he lived on Patmos in total solitude, John certainly was marooned in spiritual and societal isolation.

While stuck on that rocky island, John had the violent, apocalyptic visions that became the book of Revelation. His visions are permeated with fear of the future, anger at the corruption of the Roman Empire, and despair over the lukewarm devotion of the Christian churches. John's isolation and captivity likely fueled his urgency and intensity. Somehow, the movement of the Holy Spirit and John's immobility combined to create a series of brutal but fantastic revelations about the reality of the world and the cosmos that, in the end, all belongs to God.

Whatever political agitating John was doing before he got to Patmos, it's not likely that he did much writing. John's writing is in clumsy, almost illiterate Greek; his first language was probably Aramaic or Hebrew. Writing out a revelation from God was likely something he did because he felt he *must*, not because it was his particular gift or craft. (It is highly unlikely John of Patmos wrote the Gospel or letters of John, which are in beautiful, nearly flawless Greek.) John wasn't well educated, but, clearly, he was a passionate believer in Jesus, and probably a Jew, because he knew his Hebrew Bible and the prophets well. Instead of worrying about how good a writer he was, he threw caution to the Aegean winds and wrote his visions down in the *lingua franca* of his time so that it would be readable by not just his fellow Jews but also other Christians in the empire.

John had the drive to follow the call he felt from God to spend his imprisonment creating something that would comfort and guide others. Despair or anguish from his solitude didn't get the upper hand; he was able to work, to write, and to transmit his visions from God into a text that could be shared with others, even those far away in space and time. The book he wrote has produced great controversy ever since, but it has also remained a source of comfort, inspiration, and amazement for many.

Questions for Reflection

1. What do you imagine would be the most difficult struggle for you, physically or emotionally, if you were imprisoned? (Or, if you have had this experience, what was the most painful or humiliating aspect of it for you?)
2. When you have struggled alone, have you ever written something or made art to work through the struggle? Was it ever something you felt you could share with others going through a similar struggle?
3. If you have never done this and had an opportunity to in the future, what medium would you choose? (Writing, drawing, collage-making, music, a play, a sculpture, a quilt . . . ?)

WEDNESDAY: SOLITARY CONFINEMENT

He was despised and rejected by others;
  a man of suffering and acquainted with infirmity;
and as one from whom others hide their faces
  he was despised, and we held him of no account.

  — Isaiah 53:3

A bruised reed he will not break,
  and a dimly burning wick he will not quench;
he will faithfully bring forth justice.

  — Isaiah 42:3

Nelson Mandela recalled about the time he spent in solitary confinement, "I found solitary confinement the most forbidding aspect of prison life. There is no end and no beginning; there is only one's mind, which can begin to play tricks. Was that a dream or did it really happen? One begins to question everything."[4] Solitary confinement is a kind of death; but it is not like dying to self—the ancient way of describing a life surrendered to God—a life is seized from the most basic human normality and the self is slowly but surely eroded and erased.

There is nothing inspiring about solitary confinement, except perhaps that human beings can survive it. Many do not; according to the organization Solitary Watch, rates of suicide and self-harm are as much as thirty-three times higher than in the general prisoner population. Inmates are kept in cells eight by ten feet or smaller for twenty-three hours a day. They can hear other inmates screaming and pounding the walls. There's a single slot in the door for meals and communication. Lights are on twenty-four hours a day. There's one hour a day for exercise, and no contact with friends or family except through Plexiglas.

Reading materials, media, and even photos of loved ones are tightly monitored or not allowed.[5]

The torture of solitary confinement isn't just the isolation but a loss of the most basic means of human flourishing: a connection to the natural world, some means for choice, physical fellowship, and chances to learn and change. Judith Vasquez scraped away at the plastic sealing around her cell window with her bare fingernails for months, trying to get to the fresh air on the other side.[6] Five Muallimm-Ak said about his 2,054 days in solitary: "I was out of sight and invisible to other human beings—and eventually, even to myself."[7] Jesse Wilson wrote, "Books help me escape better than my words could ever explain. But most of all it's the love of my family, the memories of beauty, and the knowledge of humanity [that kept me going]."[8]

Solitary confinement doesn't offer a solitude of redemption—only of penance, and not even that, since penance is something freely chosen. Penance and solitude are supposed to make us better human beings, not crush us. Jesus spent a few hours in solitary confinement himself, but the men and women thrown away by our society to solitary confinement embody the abandonment and torture of his crucifixion more acutely than perhaps any other population in North America. Solitary confinement is not punishment but obliteration.

In Holy Week, as the Church turns to face into the dark winds of the crucifixion, we recall that God descended to the very depths of human suffering and abandonment. Let us remember that Christ died to redeem humankind from sin, not to tell us to continuously suffer for it, and let us remember and pray for our brothers and sisters hanging on to the edge of life in their solitary cells. Let us pray in solitude and solidarity.

Questions for Reflection

1. Do you have an opinion about the use of solitary confinement in our prison system? What do you think about it?

2. What is the closest prison to where you live? Do you know much about it? Do you ever pray for the prisoners, warden, or guards there?

MAUNDY THURSDAY: ALONE TOGETHER

For you have died, and your life is hidden with Christ in God. When Christ who is your life is revealed, then you also will be revealed with him in glory.

—Colossians 3:3–4

Today, you bring the fruits of the solitude you have practiced this Lent to the most holy days of the Christian year. Whether you've done all the practices, or haven't been able to do as many as you would have liked, or haven't done any of them, God in Christ will welcome you.

Attending the worship services of Holy Week can transform your life. The intimacy with your fellow worshipers and with Jesus through his passion is unmatched in the rest of the Christian year. Christians sit together in shared solitude, a sense of loneliness in the midst of community, each a member of the body of Christ but simultaneously standing irreconcilably apart from Christ as he is betrayed, arrested, tried, and crucified. The congregation stands alone together, like the women at the foot of the cross.

Jesus was abandoned by his friends when he was arrested. He died alone. He freely chose this last wilderness and nadir of solitude, but he was still lonely, crying out, "My God, my God, why have you forsaken me?" (Matt. 27:46). God was with him (*was* him) and yet achingly separate.

There is something of the shadow of death in the practice of solitude. In the Gospel of John, Jesus says, "unless a grain of wheat falls into the earth and dies, it remains just a single grain" (John 12:24), not denying that in its falling and dying the grain is still "single" and still alone. When we are in solitude, we open a window to death; we are choosing to be alone, in ourselves, unseen and unengaged by any other but God. If we are seen and known only by God, do we still exist? Christians do not believe that death means being lost, alone, or obliterated. There will be a loss of the life we know, certainly, but also new and eternal life in Christ. There will be oneness with God too, which perhaps we can glimpse in any moment of solitude.

To know true joy, we must know something about suffering. To know true community, we need to know something about solitude. To know that we are alive, we need to breathe in the truth of death. To know and receive the resurrection, we must first face and receive the crucifixion. Participating in the services of Holy Week is a submersion—of body, mind, and soul—in the life and heart of Jesus on his last days of life on earth and in his death. Like the waters of baptism, we go through Christ from life into death, and so to resurrection. This Holy Week, may you be buried with Christ in his death, may you share in his resurrection, and may you be reborn in him by the Holy Spirit.[9]

Questions for Reflection

1. What has been your experience of Holy Week in the past? Have you attended one or more Holy Week services before? If so, what is one you remember as particularly moving? If not, what has kept you away?
2. What has been your most intimate experience of death? How did it change your experience of life? Of solitude?
3. What has been your relationship with the cross and death of Christ? Does considering it in the light of

solitude, in both your life and Christ's, change your understanding?

GOOD FRIDAY FASTING: BEHOLD THE CROSS

Then came Jesus forth, wearing the crown of thorns, and the purple robe. And Pilate saith unto them, Behold the man!
—John 19:5 (KJV)

When they look on the one whom they have pierced, they shall mourn for him, as one mourns for an only child, and weep bitterly over him, as one weeps over a firstborn.
—Zechariah 12:10b

But all his acquaintances, including the women who had followed him from Galilee, stood at a distance, watching these things.
—Luke 23:49

Inspiration

Offer the emptiness, solitude, and pain of this fast as a deepening in your body, mind, and soul, of the grace and mystery of the cross and crucifixion. If you're not able to attend a service today, find a moment in solitude to pray Psalm 22, either silently or aloud.

Practice

Fast from one or two two meals. Do not snack. Eat and drink as simply as possible otherwise, avoiding (if not already): meat, dairy, alcohol, and sweets. *If there is any reason fasting from food may not be good for your health, do not fast.* If at all possible, do not announce or reveal your fast to others outside your immediate family, if even them.

Questions for Reflection

1. How did fasting affect your experience of Good Friday or your relationship to the cross?
2. Did it help you deepen in solitude and solidarity with Christ and his passion, or was it just inconvenient?

HOLY SATURDAY ALMSGIVING: CAPTIVES

I was in prison and you visited me.
—Matthew 25:36c

When they came to the place that is called The Skull, they crucified Jesus there with the criminals, one on his right and one on his left.
—Luke 23:33

Choose the form of almsgiving you will practice this week or, if it gives you joy, do both. Give an amount that feels generous and "hurts" a little in the context of your weekly expenses. Grow in solitude by giving to others.

1. Give cash away to someone who asks you for it.
2. Mail a check or give online to an organization that serves or advocates for people in the prison system. Prisoners are considered throwaway people, who deserve to be miserable and dehumanized. Jesus invited the criminals crucified on either side of him into the kingdom

of God. He said that when we visit someone in prison, we visit him too. Inmates may be dangerous, guilty, and vicious people, but they are as worthy of a chance at new life as anyone else. As human beings, we are all guilty of the murder of Jesus. As Christians, we can't advocate for criminal justice that is punishment without any chance for repentance or redemption. In Christ, justice and accountability are not irrelevant, but neither are there any people who can be considered disposable or unworthy of salvation. Make a gift of alms this Holy Week to an organization that does this difficult work:

— a local organization that helps ex-prisoners readjust to life in society and from reoffending

— an organization that advocates against the unjust use, or any use, of solitary confinement in the national prison system

— an organization that advocates internationally for prisoners of conscience and against the use of torture

Questions for Reflection

1. Does generosity make you feel richer or poorer this week? Does it feel like a spiritual act?
2. How did you choose where to give your alms this week?
3. Did giving make more space within you for the presence of God? How?

EASTER SUNDAY: MARY MAGDALENE AT THE TOMB

She turned around and saw Jesus standing there, but she did not know that it was Jesus. Jesus said to her, "Woman, why are you weeping? Whom are you looking for?" Supposing him to be the gardener, she said to him, "Sir, if you have carried him away, tell me where you have laid him, and I will take him away." Jesus said to her, "Mary!" She turned and said to him in Hebrew, "Rabbouni!" (which means Teacher). Jesus said to her, "Do not hold on to me, because I have not yet ascended to the Father. But go to my brothers and say to them, 'I am ascending to my Father and your Father, to my God and your God.'" Mary Magdalene went and announced to the disciples, "I have seen the Lord"; and she told them that he had said these things to her.

—John 20:14b–18

True solitude is the home of the person. . . .
Go into the desert not to escape other men, but in order to find them in God.

—Thomas Merton, *New Seeds of Contemplation*

The brutal loneliness of the cross was transformed in the holy solitude of the empty tomb. Somehow, in the silent emptiness of a tomb cut in rock, Christ came alive. God resurrected his body, wounds intact, and he took life and breath again.

When Mary Magdalene met Jesus at the tomb, however, she didn't recognize him. The two male disciples with her had come and gone, but she lingered, looking at the tomb and weeping. In that moment of solitude, two angels appeared, and she turned around and all but crashed into Jesus, standing right there with her in the garden. It wasn't until he called her by name that she knew who he was. From lonely grieving, she turned to *exhilaration*! I imagine her instinctively reaching out to grab and hug him, fierce person that she was, when Jesus said to her, "Do not hold on to me" (John 20:17). Was he telling her, literally, "Let go of me," or "Don't get too excited because I won't be with you like this much longer"? Regardless, he was trying to explain that their relationship was going to change. Instead of focusing so intently on her personal relationship with him, he was asking Mary to see their relationship in terms of her relationship with other people. He was asking her to face outward, instead of only toward him: "Do not hold onto me . . . but go to my brothers." From an intimate moment in solitude together, he calls her to proclaim what she had seen and heard to the other disciples. Legend says she not only did that but traveled as far as Ephesus and Rome,[10] perhaps even Marseilles and Egypt, repeating her famous testimony: "I have seen the Lord."

We, too, are called from our moments of solitude with God to turn outward: to love and serve others, to share the good news, to live from hospitality, justice, and mercy. In the end, our home in God is a solitude, in life and death, a holy solitude that leads us to not only a deeper inward life but also a deeper and more loving outer life. This will look different for each one of us, but we go into solitude, as Thomas Merton knew so well and put it so perfectly, "not to escape other men, but in order to find them in God."

Questions for Reflection

1. How has your experience or understanding of solitude changed this Lent?
2. How have you felt fed by solitude? What kinds of solitude have been most life-giving for you?
3. This Easter season, consider if there are new ways God may be calling you to serve others, from the deep well of love you can receive in solitude with Christ. Do you already have some hunches as to what that may be?

ACKNOWLEDGMENTS

To the sisters and oblate community of Holy Wisdom Monastery, for living into Christ through the Rule of St. Benedict, for providing a community with generous room for solitude, and for many, many blessed times of retreat.

To so many colleagues who have urged me on, first invited me to speak to their congregations, and otherwise inspired me, especially Bradley Pace, Jarrett Kerbel, Stacy Alan, Bob Wyatt, Peg Williams, Travis and Marti Stanley, Sarah Fisher Brady, Ed Bird, Kara Wagner Scherer, Kristin White, and Emily Mellott.

To Jessica Miller Kelley, Julie Tonini, and Barbara Dick, my editors.

To the "Reverent Writers," Katherine Willis Pershey, Bromleigh McClenaghan, Lee Hull Moses, Erica Schemper, and Jenn Moland-Kovash, my best cheerleaders, who are full of wisdom, courage, and good humor. I would not be here without you.

To my in-laws, who I am pretty sure have bought more copies of my books than anyone else, for themselves and to give away, especially Kate, Dan and Diana, Nancy, Becky, and Gram and Papa.

To my brother Jon, for keeping his big sister humble but always sharing fun and love, and to his wife Laurie — your hospitality rivals the Benedictines.

To Harold Jon and Giuliana Ruth, for joy, curiosity, and the gift of being themselves. For saying on Christmas morning: "More books? Are the rest of these gifts *all books*?" Welcome to the family, kids.

To Dad, for being my first editor and teaching me to take criticism, for demonstrating a life of faith almost perfectly balanced between mind, spirit, and church going, and most recently, for returning to his own writing and sharing his work with me, making the circle round.

To Mom, who said about everything she read that I have written since I was nine years old: "Heidi, this is so *good*!" For showing me how fun it is to get truly excited about books and so many other things, and for teaching me that it is okay to go off by yourself and rest awhile, even if others are disappointed. I miss you so much but know you are always with me.

To Adam, for everything.

APPENDIX A

TEN WAYS TO
BE SILENT

Adapted from a post to my old blog,
"The Vicar of Bolingbrook," in Lent 2015

The mind is a busy, chatty place; your body can be silent, but your mind is different. Your mind needs a way to anchor itself in the silence so that you can relax into the stillness and warmth of God's love instead of drifting away to think about dinner or the right snappy comeback.

Experiment with silence if you haven't before, or if you have and find yourself longing for more, here are things that have worked for me:

1. Look out of a window with an interesting view and watch what you see.
2. Repeat a word to yourself. The ancients recommended words of one syllable: love, grace, peace. I've also been well fed by longer words: Jesus, Spirit, mercy. No need to be a martinet about this; your word or mantra is to bring you back to focusing on God's love, not to be an end in itself.

3. Follow your breathing. You can focus on breathing in and out around the syllables of one of the above words or a short prayer. I have used:
   a. God / is love. (breathe in / breathe out)
   b. Jesus Christ / Son of God / have mercy / on me.
   c. Spirit / come.
4. Sit and just let your mind wander. Try not to worry, plan, or regret. If/When you do, bring yourself back to the presence of God, a prayer, or a word (like those suggested above).
5. Pray with your body. Try to feel each part, on the outside and the inside, and say to each one: "God loves you," starting with your toes, working your way up to your fingertips, and up to the top of your head.
6. Drive in silence. Notice how it's different from listening to music or talk radio. Notice if you crave noise while you drive, and what that feels like. Do you notice different things around you? Does anything surface in your mind as you drive that might not have if you were listening to something else?
7. In silence, take a nap. To make a full sleep cycle, it's best to have twenty minutes, forty minutes, or an hour for this, so you don't just feel more exhausted. Sleeping can be a wonderful way to let go and let God love you.
8. Take a pen, pencil, or marker and let your mind wander and doodle, in silence, for one to five minutes.
9. Try to descend your mind into your heart. What does that mean? I'm not always sure; I learned this phrase from Henri Nouwen and Eastern Orthodox teachings on prayer. I try to focus awareness on my heart and my breathing, to open myself up, let go, and let God pray in me. (I'm not sure what that means either, exactly.)
10. Try centering prayer: strive to empty your mind and simply sit in God's loving presence for twenty min-

utes. This is hard. It's a good way to practice failing at something, honestly. There is a lot of help in other places, should you want to practice it more—see the Further Reading section for suggestions.

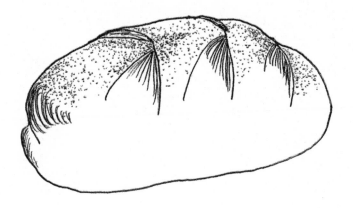

APPENDIX B

RECIPES

EASY LITTLE BREAD

A quick bread recipe to make for someone in need; I have made this many times.

1¼ cups / 300 ml warm water (105–115°F)
2 teaspoons active dry yeast (one packet)
1 tablespoon runny honey (or maple syrup)
1 cup / 4.5 oz. / 125 g unbleached all-purpose flour
1 cup / 5 oz. / 140 g whole wheat flour
1 cup / 3.5 oz. / 100 g rolled oats (not instant oats)
1½ teaspoons fine grain sea salt
2 tablespoons butter, melted, for brushing

In a medium bowl, sprinkle the yeast onto the warm water and stir until the yeast dissolves. Stir in the honey and set aside for a few minutes, until the yeast blooms and swells a bit: 5–10 minutes. In the meantime, mix the flours, oats, and salt in a large bowl. Add the wet mixture to the dry and stir very well. Brush an 8-cup loaf pan generously with some of the melted butter. Turn the dough into the tin, cover with a clean, slightly damp cloth, and set in a warm place for 30 minutes, to rise.

Preheat the oven to 350°, with a rack in the middle. When ready, brush with butter and bake the bread for 35–40 minutes, until golden and pulling away from the sides of the pan. I finish things up by leaving the bread under the broiler for just a heartbeat, to give the top a bit deeper color. Remove from oven, and turn the bread out of the pan quickly. Let it cool on a rack so that it doesn't steam in the pan. Serve warm, slathered with butter. Makes one loaf.

SOURCE: The blog, "101 Cookbooks," by Heidi Swanson (http://www.101cookbooks.com/); adapted from *Gran's Kitchen: Recipes from the Notebooks of Dulcie May Booker*, by Natalie Oldfield

DYING RED EASTER EGGS

An alternate Easter egg project[1] and a favorite of Mary Magdalene,[2] who tradition says lived as a desert solitary herself for a while. I made these for my church one Easter and couldn't believe how gorgeous they were.

12 white or brown eggs, at room temperature (brown eggs will be a deeper color)
12 yellow or red onions
3 tablespoons white vinegar
2 teaspoons vegetable oil
water

Clean the eggs so that there are no particles sticking to their shells. Chip or peel the dry skins from the onions. Reserve onions for another use. In a stainless steel saucepan, boil 4½ cups water, onion skins, and vinegar. When it boils, turn heat down to low and simmer, covered, for 30 minutes. Pour mixture through a strainer into another stainless steel saucepan or a steel or glass bowl and let cool.

Using a stainless steel pan with a wide diameter, arrange the room-temperature eggs in one layer. Pour the cooled dye over them.

Bring liquid to an easy boil over medium heat. Then reduce to low and cover. Simmer for 10 minutes, then start checking for color by gently raising an egg out with a slotted spoon. It may take up to 20 minutes to get the right color. Do not cook for more than 20 minutes. (If, after 20 minutes, the eggs are not a deep enough color, remove pot from heat, cool to room temperature, then place in refrigerator until desired color is reached.)

Remove eggs with a slotted spoon and cool on racks. When cool enough to handle, massage in a little olive oil to each, then polish with a paper towel. Store in refrigerator until you hide, display, or serve them.

SOURCE: The website, "The Kitchn" (http://www.the kitchn.com/), recipe by Sara Kate Gillingham-Ryan

NOTES

Introduction

1. Richard Foster, *Celebration of Discipline*, 20th anniv. ed. (New York: HarperSanFrancisco, 1998), 96.
2. Henri Nouwen, *Out of Solitude: Three Meditations on the Christian Life* (Notre Dame: Ave Maria, 2004), 26.
3. Walter Brueggemann, *Sabbath as Resistance: Saying No to the Culture of Now, New Edition with Study Guide* (Louisville, KY: Westminster John Knox, 2017), 10.
4. *The Book of Common Prayer*, 265.

Preparing for Lent

1. Widely attributed to Saint Theophan the Recluse, 1815–1894, a Russian Orthodox scholar, priest, and monk who lived as a hermit from the age of fifty-one to his death.

Week 1: Solitude and Silence

1. Regis J. Armstrong, J. A. Wayne Hellmann, William J. Short, eds., *Francis of Assisi: Early Documents, Volume 2* (Hyde Park, NY: New City Press, 2000), 215.
2. Teresa of Avila, *The Interior Castle*, trans. Mirabai Starr (New York: Riverhead Books, 2003), 45.
3. Thomas Merton, *New Seeds of Contemplation* (New York: New Directions, 1961), 1.

4. "The Sacraments," *The Book of Common Prayer* (1979), 857.

5. Thomas Merton, *New Seeds of Contemplation* (New York: New Directions, 1961), 82–83.

6. Ruth Burrows, OCD, *Essence of Prayer* (Mahwah, NJ: Paulist Press, 2006), 1, italics original.

7. See Deuteronomy 13.

8. Teresa of Calcutta, *Come Be My Light: The Private Writings of the Saint of Calcutta*, ed. Brian Kolodiejchuk (New York: Doubleday, 2007), 187.

9. Shūsaku Endō, *Silence* (New York: Picador, 2016), 183.

10. Catherine Doherty, *Poustinia: Encountering God in Solitude, Silence and Prayer* (Combermere, ON: Madonna House, 1993), 51.

Week 2: Solitude and Struggle

1. Evagrius Ponticus, 345–399 BCE an Egyptian monk and hermit known for his teachings on prayer.

2. Antony the Great, 251–356 BCE (his last words), from Saint Athanasius, "Antony's Last Will," *The Life of St. Antony*, http://www.patristics.co/on-the-life-of-st-anthony/.

3. Ibid., "Birth and Beginnings."

4. Ibid., "Early Conflicts with the Devil."

5. African American Spiritual and song of the civil rights movement.

6. Famously used by Bianca Del Rio on the television series *RuPaul's Drag Race*.

7. Notably of Stephen in Acts 7:54–60.

Week 3: Solitude and Journeys

1. Saint Augustine of Hippo, 354–430 BCE, a North African bishop, theologian, and author of the first Christian autobiography, *Confessions*.

2. Vinita Hampton Wright, "Four Principles of Pilgrimage," *Days of Deepening Friendship* (blog), July 27, 2015, http://deepeningfriendship.loyolapress.com/?s=four+principles+of+pilgrimage.

3. *John of the Mountains: The Unpublished Journals of John Muir*, ed. Linnie Marsh Wolfe (Madison: University of Wisconsin Press, 1979), 439.

4. Prayer of Azariah (additions to the book of Daniel), vv. 49–50.

5. Henry David Thoreau, "Walking," *The Atlantic*, June 1862, https://www.theatlantic.com/magazine/archive/1862/06 /walking/304674/.

6. George McLeod, quoted in Ronald Ferguson, *Chasing the Wild Goose: The Story of the Iona Community* (Glasgow, Scotland: Wild Goose Publications, 1998), 65.

7. Traditionally attributed to John Chrysostom, 349–407 BCE, Turkish bishop, theologian, and a hermit for a short while.

8. Aiden Owen, OHC, "Learning How to Fast," *Grounding in the Spirit* (blog), November 20, 2016, https://groundinginthespirit .wordpress.com.

9. Ibid.

Week 4: Solitude and Hospitality

1. Catherine Doherty, *Poustinia: Encountering God in Solitude, Silence and Prayer* (Combermere ON: Madonna House, 1993), 23.

2. Ibid.

3. Gregory the Great, *Life and Miracles of St. Benedict* (Collegeville MN: Liturgical Press, n.d.), 4.

4. Amy Frykholm, *Julian of Norwich* (Brewster, MA: Paraclete Press, 2010), 76.

5. Julian of Norwich, *Revelations of Divine Love*, ch. 61, pp. 152–53.

6. *The Book of Margery Kempe*, originally dictated in Middle English in the 1430s by a mother of fourteen who owned a brewery and went on many travels. Available from many publishers, in the original and in several modern English translations.

7. When Simeon prophesied about the baby Jesus, Luke says, "the child's father and mother were amazed at what was being said about him" (2:33).

8. Simone Weil and Joë Bousquet, *Correspondance* (Lausanne: l'Age d'Homme, 1982), 18.

9. Simone Weil, *Gravity and Grace* (New York: Routledge Classics, 1999), 17.

10. H. G. Bohn, *Handbook of Proverbs* (1855) as quoted in Lynne Babb, *Fasting: Spiritual Freedom beyond Our Appetites* (Downers Grove, IL: Intervarsity, 2006), 64.

11. Augustine of Hippo, as quoted in Scot McKnight, *Fasting*, The Ancient Practices Series (Nashville: Thomas Nelson, 2009), 105.

12. McKnight, *Fasting*, 108.

Week 5: Solitude and Resistance

1. Seraphim of Sarov, 1754–1833, Russian monk and *startsy* (hermit).

2. *Quotations of Martin Luther King Jr.* (Bedford MA: Applewood Books, 2004), 26.

3. Howard Thurman, *Jesus and the Disinherited* (Boston: Beacon Press, 1976), 11.

4. Quoted in *Papers of Martin Luther King Jr.*, vol. 6, ed. Clayborne Carson and Susan Carson (Berkeley: University of California, 2007), 299.

5. Howard Thurman, interview by Landrum Bolling, "Knowledge of the Love of the Lord," *Conversations with Howard Thurman*, Howard Thurman Educational Trust, 1978, YouTube video, 56:38, posted by Mischa Scorer, August 27, 2015, https://www.youtube.com/watch?v=KvJVxsezAwc.

6. Howard Thurman, *With Head and Heart: The Autobiography of Howard Thurman* (New York: Harcourt Brace, 1979), 7, italics original.

7. Ibid., 255.

8. Ali Merad, *Christian Hermit in an Islamic World: A Muslim's View of Charles de Foucauld*, trans. Zoe Hersov (New York: Paulist Press, 1999), 82.

9. Peter France, *Hermits: The Insights of Solitude* (London: Chatto and Windus, 1996), 155.

Holy Week: Solitude and Confinement

1. See also Malachi 3:1–3.

2. It was a popular enough plot that the story was told again in what became the book of Bel and the Dragon, found in the Apocrypha and in the Roman Catholic Bible.

3. See also Acts 6:5.
4. Nelson Mandela, *Long Walk to Freedom* (New York: Back Bay Books, 1994), 416.
5. For more information, see "FAQ," Solitary Watch, http://solitarywatch.com/.
6. Jean Casella, James Ridgeway, and Sarah Shourd, eds., *Hell Is a Very Small Place: Voices from Solitary Confinement* (New York: The New Press, 2016), 57.
7. Ibid., 148.
8. Ibid., 82.
9. *The Book of Common Prayer*, 306—from the liturgy of Holy Baptism, where the priest blesses the water with these words: "In it we are buried with Christ in his death. By it we share in his resurrection. Through it we are reborn by the Holy Spirit."
10. Could she be the "Mary" greeted by Paul in Romans 16:6, his letter to the Christians in that city?

Appendix B: Recipes

1. Dying Easter eggs red is an old tradition in the Orthodox Church. I use onion skins, and they turn the eggs a beautiful, dark, brownish red—a bit fiercer than the usual Easter pink or yellow.
2. In Orthodox tradition, the story is told that a few years after Jesus' resurrection, Mary Magdalene came before Tiberius Caesar. Anyone who appeared before the emperor was to bring a gift, and Mary Magdalene came holding an egg in her hand and saying in greeting, "Christ is Risen!" Tiberius responded, "How can anyone rise from the dead? That is as impossible as that egg in your hand turning red!" And the white egg in her hand turned a deep, dark red.

FURTHER READING

Websites

Contempative   Outreach — https://www.contemplative
outreach.org/

Hermitary — http://www.hermitary.com/ : Resources and
reflections on hermits and solitude — articles, reviews,
features, and blogs about hermits in lore, literature, history (East and West), art, film; solitude, silence, and
simplicity.

Raven's Bread Hermit Ministries — http://www.ravens
breadministries.com/: Food for those in solitude. (See
also their book below, *Consider the Ravens*, based on the
newsletter that preceded the site.)

Books

Holy Solitude — Solitaries and Hermits

Cadwallader, Robyn. *The Anchoress*. New York: Picador,
2016.

Doherty, Catherine. *Poustinia: Encountering God in Solitude,
Silence and Prayer*. Combermere ON: Madonna House,
1993.

France, Peter. *Hermits: The Insights of Solitude*. London:
Chatto and Windus, 1996.

Fredette, Paul A. and Karen Karper Fredette. *Consider the Ravens: On Contemporary Hermit Life*. Bloomington, IN: iUniverse, 2011.

Frykholm, Amy. *Julian of Norwich*. Brewster, MA: Paraclete Press, 2010.

Jones, W. Paul. *Teaching the Dead Bird to Sing*. Brewster, MA: Paraclete Press, 2002.

Karper, Karen. *Where God Begins to Be: A Woman's Journey into Solitude*. Lincoln: iUniverse, 2004.

Kirk, Connie Ann. *Emily Dickinson: A Biography*. Westport, CT: Greenwood Press, 2004.

Maitland, Sara. *A Book of Silence*. Berkeley: Counterpoint, 2008.

Nicolson, Adam. *Sea Room: An Island Life in the Hebrides*. New York: Harper, 2007.

Ross, Maggie. *Seasons of Death and Life: A Wilderness Memoir*. New York: Harper, 1990.

Holy Solitude within Community

Furlong, Monica. *Merton: A Biography*. Liguori, MO: Liguori, 1995.

Godden, Rumer. *In This House of Brede*. Loyola Classics. Chicago: Loyola Press, 2005 (a novel).

Maguire, Nancy Klein. *An Infinity of Little Hours: Five Young Men and Their Trial of Faith in the Western World's Most Austere Monastic Order*. New York: PublicAffairs, 2006.

Martin, Valerie. *Salvation: Scenes from the Life of St. Francis*. New York: Knopf, 2001.

Moorhouse, Geoffrey. *Sun Dancing*. San Diego: Harcourt Brace, 1997 (about Skellig Michael).

Norris, Kathleen. *The Cloister Walk*. New York: Riverhead Books, 1996.

Nouwen, Henri. *The Genesee Diary: Report from a Trappist Monastery*. New York: Doubleday, 1976.

Practicing Prayer in Solitude

Burrrows, Ruth, OCD. *Essence of Prayer*. Mahwah, NJ: Paulist Press, 2006.

Doherty, Catherine. *Poustinia: Encountering God in Solitude, Silence and Prayer.* Combermere, ON: Madonna House, 1993.

Hall, Thelma. *Too Deep for Words: Rediscovering Lectio Divina.* New York: Paulist Press, 1988.

Keating, Thomas. *Intimacy with God: An Introduction to Centering Prayer.* New York: Crossroad Publishing: 2009.

Laird, Martin. *Into the Silent Land.* New York: Oxford UP, 2006.

Teresa of Avila. *The Interior Castle.* Translated by Mirabai Starr. New York: Riverhead, 2004.

Fasting

Babb, Lynne. *Fasting: Spiritual Freedom beyond Our Appetites.* Downers Grove, IL: Intervarsity, 2006.

McKnight, Scot. *Fasting.* The Ancient Practices Series. Nashville: Thomas Nelson, 2009.

Film

Into Great Silence (Le Grand Silence). Directed by Philip Gröning. Quebec: Mongrel Media, 2007.

A glimpse of the lives of the monk-hermits of Le Grande Chartreuse, oldest monastery of the Carthusian order. From the official description: "Phillip Gröning, sans crew or artificial lighting, lived in the monks' quarters for six months filming their daily prayers, tasks, rituals, and rare outdoor excursions. . . . It has no score, no voiceover, and no archival footage. What remains is stunningly elemental: time, space, and light."